New Models
for Church
Administration

Dr. Raymond B. Knudsen is the author of

NEW MODELS FOR FINANCING THE LOCAL
  CHURCH
NEW MODELS FOR CREATIVE GIVING
THE TRINITY
MODELS FOR MINISTRY
DEVELOPING DYNAMIC STEWARDSHIP

New Models
for Church
Administration

*The Practical Application of
Business Principles*

RAYMOND B. KNUDSEN

Association Press
𝒻 Follett Publishing Company/Chicago

Designed by Donna Cook and Karen Yops

Library of Congress Cataloging in Publication Data
Knudsen, Raymond B.
  New models for church administration.
  Includes index.
  1. Church management. I. Title.
BV652.K58   254   79-11908
ISBN 0-695-81254-8

First Printing

Dedicated to my brother
BENJAMIN FRANKLIN KNUDSEN
a businessperson fully
dedicated to
humanitarian services

Contents

Preface

Why is it that good businesspersons lose all business sense when they get behind stained glass windows?

Many have asked that question and what some persons affirm may be true. Actually, they have never had a chance. They may have indeed been overpowered by the ecclesia.

The tragedy in the history of the Christian church is the fact that it has not operated on proper business principles.

In *New Models for Financing the Local Church* we took models from the world of finance and applied them to financial development in the local church.

In *New Models for Creative Giving* we took models from the world of philanthropy and applied them to Christian stewardship and individual resourcefulness to fund ministry and mission.

In *New Models for Church Administration* we choose to lift models from the world of business and apply them to the administration of the local church and its related agencies.

We pray that this book may meet with as great enthusiasm and effectiveness as have the two volumes preceding it.

Raymond B. Knudsen

New Models
for Church
Administration

1

Basic Tenets
Common to
Business and Religion

Traveling across the United States today, one is impressed with the significance of commerce.

Trade centers dwarf church steeples.

Mercantile towers and shopping malls form the hubs of communities.

Business has come of age, and our society is geared to a world of commerce and industry.

Six basic tenets form the foundation for the business-oriented society.

1. That its products, its commodities, and its services are significant and important.

In the world of business, the worth of life and the success of individuals are judged by clear and measurable standards. What one has. What one is able to buy. How much more one has this year than last year. The fact that one is not only able to possess many things but that these many things are up-to-date and of the most popular design and fashion is of great importance. Manufacturers have been able to program into their design patterns of obsolescence in order that persons will buy next year, and/or the following year, simply because styles have changed even before the product has worn out or ceased to become functional.

2. That interpersonal relationships are vitally important.

Business senses the importance of interpersonal relationships and the significance of producing models and designs complimentary to persons and types. One need not look very long in the advertising sections of our newspapers and magazines to discover that a fundamental technique of advertising is to project an image of individual types utilizing a design, endorsing a product, and implying that the advertised matter will not only be acceptable but desirable in the consumer market. In purchasing the product, an individual identifies with the values and capabilities projected by the person or persons in the advertisement.

3. That the projection of a corporate image is essential.

Corporate structures are sometimes international, frequently national, and at least regional. The trade names on products are identifiable in the urban, suburban, and rural areas. And where merchandising is limited because of the size or remoteness of a community, the mail order catalog, with products and services as close as one's telephone, is the instrument for marketing. We could mention a dozen institutional/trade/product names, and in each case product identification would emerge with so strong an image that the corporate and product images are inseparable.

4. That goals are significant.

Corporations establish goals based on surveys that have been made to determine the market. In each one computations are made concerning what each considers its fair share of the market, and calculations are made concerning marketing feasibility (which includes production, packaging, and the per-foot and per-person cost in selling the product). Surveys are conducted and limited marketing experience is tested in order to ensure the feasibility of the project and the certainty of attaining objectives that will strengthen the corporate structure and provide reasonable profitability through the commercial enterprise.

5. That a structured concept of values is instrumental in meeting goals.

Social acceptance, community standing, personal significance, and affluence are the virtues projected, and life's values are measured in terms of applications made by individuals to values that may be of far greater virtue and worth to the manufacturer and marketing persons than to the consumer and user. Through mass media, commerce emphasizes the concepts of value, and individual consumers become convinced that the values of the marketplace are certainly the values to be assumed and acclaimed in every other place as well.

6. That the world has a future of promise and hope.

Business does not necessarily strive for a city whose builder and maker is God, but certainly the thrust is toward a world where commerce and industry are influential and each person is capable of buying practically everything that is produced. The end goal is not only for every person to have everything that is produced but for every person to have the most current model, so that he or she may be fully accepted as a contemporary individual.

The basic tenets underlying the development of religion in the United States are not so different from those underlying business and industry as might at first appear.

There was a generation that came to these shores with a faith that organized churches. Their hopes, dreams, and aspirations were sky-high, and the spires and towers that they built overshadowed their businesses and their residences. Not only did they build houses for worship, but they also built classrooms for instruction, auditoriums for inspiration, and laboratories for the testing of the height and depth, length and breadth of the missionary enterprise. And because they believed that the firstfruits of their lives belonged to God, they accomplished the evidence of things yet seen on our continent; and because they believed that the firstfruits of their common witness belonged to God, they accomplished the evidence of things yet seen in practically every country of the world! Their missionaries planted the cross in fertile soil, and one cannot visit a single land without seeing churches, schools, hospitals, clinics, and mission stations that bear testimony to this zeal.

Let us consider the six comparable tenets in the realm of the religious.

1. That faith in God is of vital significance.

Although it is true that the generation of the church founders was less enlightened than this generation, more superstitious than this generation, and less knowledgeable than this generation, they acknowledged a faith in a providential God. They would not risk the possibility that there was no God or Divine Providence to govern their ways. The risk of faith was a better choice than the risk of doubt. Having made this decision, they supported the choice with their substance.

The ancient Israelites came to a sacred place of decision and choice and erected pillars of stone. The later Christian pioneers did so also. Their pillars were cathedrals in the cities, churches in the towns, and chapels in the open country. Out of either faith or fear they gave evidence to their convictions of providence on every frontier.

2. That the development of interpersonal relationships through fellowship is basic.

The church became the hub for the circumference of community, and the sense of relatedness and concern grew out of it. Each person was dependent upon, and benefited from, the talents of others, and the pooling of resources through a barter system made for both survival and progress. Talents and resources went beyond the requirements for lodging and foodstuffs as the professionals and paraprofessionals brought to the community their gifts and skills making possible health, education, and social services. Practically none took root without the involvement of the church.

While service organizations began as programs of social concern in the local church, most spun off to become independent agencies. Some even developed a national connectional system to make a more effective organization at the local level and provide brokerage services for personnel, program, and the sharing of experiences. Some continued a relationship with the denomination structure but, for all practical purposes, are actually indigenous unto themselves.

3. That an institutional structure lends credibility to the cause of religion.

Throughout the Old Testament one is mindful of the fact that the political structure in the Judaic tradition was basically an ecclesiastical structure. Religious bodies defined the direction that their people should go, and it was interpreted to be a theological mandate. "Thus saith the Lord" was the preamble to every constitution and each constitutional concept. And when they could not see a pillar of cloud by day or a pillar of fire by night, people could at least smell the smoke.

Following the course of history through a hundred and twenty generations, the blueprint hardly changes. The church was the focal point for government, and churchmen were the spokespersons, as accepted authorities, for almost every assembly considering a cause. Community life revolved around the church, and in many events the church evaluated situations, made judgments, and imposed penalties upon wrongdoers.

4. That goals are necessary and important.

Each person had a goal that he or she had established as a life goal—a goal that related to work, family, and future. The common goal was forged on the anvil of circumstances as small groups beat upon issues to form a matrix for the future. Not all were included in the goal-setting process, but all were affected by it. Step by step, society moved into the future, and the cluster of homes became a village, the village became a town, the town became a city, and the city became a metropolis. Interestingly enough, the city and metropolis may have been the initial objective. It seems that the unconscious movement of society is toward the urbanized culture, just as the story of humankind begins in a garden and reaches its consummation in a city. While the urban trend has produced decay and disenchantment, actually the course was one of hope and promise. Attainment would mean better homes, better schools, better community organizations, and a better way of life.

5. That a system of values is crucial.

Organizations are formed for the purpose of determining and maintaining values. The constitution, bylaws, and working agreements establish a moral and ethical code within a community that ensures the integrity of the individuals holding membership therein and establishes a social climate for those who reside in a particular area. Just as an individual is known by the company he or she keeps, a community is known by the organizations it sustains, and the strength of particular organizations emphasizes the worth of the particular values made articulate by its corporate life.

6. That lives should be dedicated to an enduring hope.

In Western civilization the focus has been upon youth. Each generation wants the economic, social, and political lot to be better for each succeeding generation. This very goal constitutes a dream (an eschatology, in technical theological parlance) that may include not only a significant goal for attainment for the benefit of succeeding generations but a goal for individual attainment for individuals in life after death. Call it personal immortality if you will. Religious organizations have a kinship to this, and historically one has difficulty in discovering any that do not include such an objective. In fact, the eschatological hope becomes the keystone in relationship to the preceding five. None would be considered of particular significance if divorced from the eternal dimension.

So here are the six basic tenets of business and of religion. If they are not identical in every respect, still they are similar enough that religion need not hesitate to examine and claim for its own purposes those elements in business experience that are relevant to its own purposes. The prodigal son may have been wandering in a far country, but some of his experiences can be examined with profit by his less adventurous brothers who have stayed at home—and whose lives are stuck in familiar ruts.

2

Administrating Purpose

What is the purpose of the church today?

Few business enterprises can survive over a long period of time without giving serious consideration to their market. Yet congregation after congregation will continue program and activities with no consideration whatever to the community that they have been chartered to serve.

Administrators and administrative bodies need to consider seriously the question, What is the purpose of the church? Market and mission will come into focus as we discover purpose.

WORSHIP

Worship is an obvious answer to the question of purpose. Most church structures were designed with worship in mind. The nave with the chancel, pulpit, and/or lectern; choir loft and baptistery or baptismal font; narthex and cloisters for assembly and greeting. Everything else was secondary to them. Actually, in most situations the sanctuary was prepared to accommodate the peak audiences at Christmas and Easter, and the average attendance at public worship today is usually little more than a shadow of that at high holy day events.

Worship is important, and the space provided for it in the church compound is indicative of the priority standing given to it. Not only is space indicative of that priority but the appointments in terms of litany, music, furnishings, and appurtenances speak of it as well. As much as 90 percent of the church's physical assets focus on the primacy of worship and the worship services. And 90 percent of the church leadership's time is assumed to serve that purpose.

We need to recognize the fact that times have changed. The local church is no longer the center for life and culture. Sunday is no longer considered by most to be the Lord's day but only a part of the weekend. While many must be gainfully employed, the vast majority consider the weekend for personal enjoyment, recreation, and opportunities not available in the workaday world. For many, worship interrupts weekend enjoyment. Services are not scheduled to accommodate individual needs.

As administrators we need to take a careful look at the times for worship as well as the time that will be required for the worship experience.

The Roman Catholic Church has made significant progress in scheduling times for the Mass. Masses on Friday and Saturday evenings, as well as during afternoon hours on other days, are certainly innovative. However, it has not shown itself so flexible with regard to the length of the celebration, which is seldom other than long and longer.

Many of us outside the business world assume that all the buying needs of people can certainly be met through five or six days each week between the hours of nine o'clock in the morning and five o'clock in the afternoon. Yet marketing seven days a week and as many as eighteen hours in each of the seven days has had a tremendous effect on the gross national product.

We need to give serious consideration to opportune times for worship and the limited schedules that may best meet the needs of those who will indeed "take time to be holy."

We must not fall into the trap of measuring the effectiveness of the schedule of services by the degree to which such services utilize the seating capacity of the facilities for worship. Because a sanctuary provides seating space for 2000 persons does not mean that worship experiences involving a dozen, fifty, or a hundred persons are not really worthwhile and are not meeting basic human needs. Commerce does not stop when it has asked how many persons are in a particular store at a particular time. Rather, it wants to know the gross business and the number of persons involved in a seven-day period.

Following a change of ministers, a midwestern church moved from two services each Sunday morning to only one. Officers contended that the seating space in the church was adequate to accommodate both groups at one time. Some were especially anxious for the single service in order that they could "get to know one another better." Still another argument was that it would be an accommodation to the musicians and soloists. After the change was made, the congregation seemed pleased. There were more people in church. In an in-depth study undertaken later, the officers discovered that attendance at the single services was 20 percent less than that for the two services. There was a direct relationship between the discontinuance of the second service and the financial crunch that was experienced in the second fiscal year that followed.

One or two services alone cannot meet the liturgical needs of people in a society of complex schedules and competitive influences. The size of the crowd in terms of the space for worship must never be the important factor. Worship must be programmed to meet the needs of people, and the church, like business, may well give consideration to the seven-day week!

The scheduled length for public worship should vary to accommodate time frames of practicality in individual schedules. A greater number should be programmed for twenty or thirty minutes.

Programming in worship is equally important.

The liturgy, lectionary, psalms, and hymns accommodate the matrix of the past to the extent that one worshiping in the church at the beginning of each quarter of this century cannot discern any difference in the program or purpose of the religious organization. In fact, if you were to take a Sunday church bulletin from a Sunday in the first year of each quarter of this century, you would be hard pressed to identify the date as 1900, 1925, 1950, or 1975.

The timelessness of religion causes us to be comfortable with this fact, and we enjoy singing "O God, our help in ages past, our hope for years to come," assuming that he is indeed the same "yesterday, today, and forever."

But times do change. And while God may be the same yesterday, today, and forever, we must comprehend the fact that humankind's understanding of him changes. This was true in the period of the patriarchs as well as that of the prophets, of the disciples as well as of the apostles, of the saints as well as of the reformers.

We need to administrate the times for worship as well as the duration of the periods given to worship and the content of the worship experience in order that each may be truly significant to the participant and provide a meaningful expression in faith to those who stand in awe of Him.

It is apparent that the church is not doing that now. It is just as obvious to one who pages through the annals of history that the church did exactly that in times past. The greatest musical compositions were written for accompaniments to worship, and the hymnody and liturgy of the church caused the religious organization to be the center of the people's lives and communities. The finest music, the best speaking, the most spectacular pageantry, and the most significant influences became integral parts of the worship event.

But this has changed. Secular activities and influences have bypassed the church. Musical compositions by modern composers do not focus upon religious themes. Folk songs have taken the place of religious verse in poetry and song. Able, young, and articulate speakers present the news and provide commentary for all types of events on radio and television. Speech writers capable of the very best in English idiom and prose provide the material for those in the public eye. Sights and sounds, with color and motion, make the stage and screen outstanding in audiovisual capability today, and improvement comes with each new year. Ministers and churches assume that they simply cannot match the quality or quantity of those competitive factors. But they at least need to come of age in projecting their purpose.

They can project purpose by interpreting their mission in contemporary language and modes of communication.

They can project their purpose by communicating their mission in new ways through which they may be understood by the emerging generation.

They can project their purpose by adapting their mission to today's problems and enabling persons to realize that the implementation of that mission really does make a difference.

They can project their purpose by penetrating society and culture with a unique contribution that effects systemic change and implements a redemptive process.

Anything less is a betrayal of purpose to an eternal responsibility for meaningful worship.

PRAYER

Prayer seems an equally good answer to the question of the purpose of the church. While prayer is invariably a part of the worship experience, it is an experience apart from worship as well.

The marketing processes in the United States are not modeled on the assumption that persons will buy all that they need at one time. A weekly shopping spree probably is still the most prevalent pattern. However, few indeed can span the time from one shopping day to the next without stopping from time to time for one thing or another. The express lanes, limited to those persons purchasing fewer than eight, ten, or twelve items, testify to this.

Comparable express lanes should be programmed in the church, throughout the day and each day of the week, in order that individuals may exercise the privilege of prayer in places prepared and dedicated for that purpose.

The most meaningful prayer is not necessarily that included in the liturgy for public worship.

Here indeed, the needle may be placed on the record and the transcription will be the same day after day, week after week, month after month, and year after year. Our Lord talked about "vain repetition." We who presume not to have it are caught in the trap, and if that is not bad enough, we conclude our petitions by reciting the petitions of those recorded by the Master's prayer pattern for the ages.

Here again, it is not the place of the administrator to assume the role of the theologian or the liturgist. However, opportunities for particular needs must be programmed and intercession periods defined in such a way that folk may gather in prayer as they seek the solution to problems and needs and make known their desires for the resolution of circumstances and situations that plague the human situation.

Prayer opportunities must be issue-oriented on occasion and the prayer purpose restricted in order that minds and bodies may be given to resolve problems and bring answer to persistent questions and needs that can come to salvation only through the religious community.

It is not enough only to administrate the opportunities. Equally important is the task of making known those solutions and reconciliations that have resulted from the prayers and devotions of those engaged in dialogue with God.

Perhaps we need a tab key on our communications instruments to record and make known the significant requisitions that have been met through dialogue with God.

WITNESSING

Witnessing can be a third answer to the question of the purpose of the church. As in worship and prayer, God appears to be available only at particular times, and there is a tendency for clergy and lay leaders to determine the times presumably most acceptable to God—and certainly most acceptable to the local leadership.

For most churches the primary witness is the attendance factor itself. Arriving and departing at the appropriate time is a public announcement of those things most earnestly believed by a person and colleagues in worship.

No organization in the world assembles as many people on a one-time-a-week basis as does the church. It has a great opportunity.

Witnessing must take place in the day-to-day workaday world as well. Actually it is there that it stands the test, and it is in those arenas that the significant witness is made and needs to be made. The exercise of the witness to faith is to live lives complimentary to the Gospel.

In the mainline churches we have been weak in providing instrumentalities, as well as training—or the know-how—to enable individuals to give witness to their faith. Many never discern the Christian witness in a person, even though a person is upright in character and considered honest and reliable by fellow workers.

Administrators may here make a unique contribution by developing and making available significant and proper instrumentalities bearing witness to the faith and heralding the importance of the Gospel in these times. Such instrumentalities are used to introduce new cars, new clothes, new furniture, and new appliances. A new understanding of the Gospel is in order, and the science of communication needs to be applied to the witnessing function in these times.

ORDERING LIVES

A fourth purpose of the church is the ordering of lives. In a sense, it is to instill in persons a code of behavior that is morally and ethically acceptable. It is interesting to see cultural change and the tendency of organized religion ultimately to conform to it. Hopefully religion has an influence on culture, but there is no question but that culture has an effect on religion. The pendulum seems to swing from one extreme to the other. Certainly there are times in the history of Christianity that the church has had the greater influence on culture. But obviously there are times when culture has had the greater influence on religion. Viewing the church in these times, we can see the influence of our culture on its faith and practice as it relates to racism, sexism, and clericalism.

While some believe that there is a sincere effort in the church to bring systemic change in these matters, there is a great effort in secularism to influence that change in the church. Those who would legislate and demonstrate are forcing their attitude and life-style on the religious society, even to the extent of retranslating the Scriptures, rewriting liturgies, and revising hymnbooks.

Instead of ordering lives in terms of morals and ethics, the church is unwillingly made to conform to influences that will change its posture—but not necessarily in time to save its strength of constituency and acceptability.

Projecting the image of ordering lives seems inconsistent with volunteerism and a free, open society. The Protestant concept of the Roman Catholic discipline for priests, nuns, monks, and brothers implies a superimposed pattern for life and practice that simply destroys individuality and the unique contribution that individuals make of their own volition at times they select through their own initiative. And in some situations projecting the ordering of lives is suggestive of militarism and the type of life-style suggested by a closed society where each is under the force of the arm and hammer.

The ordering of lives central to the ministry and mission of Jesus is consistent with the objective of pure religion in the mind of the prophet in meeting the requirements of God. "Do justly, love mercy, and walk humbly with God." To do justly is to be fair. To love mercy is to be benevolent and not overbearing or insistent of one's concepts or way.

To walk humbly with God is to complement the divine way in an existence that weaves the lives of people in a fabric of universal human family relationships.

A witness is conviction! Certainty! Creative influence! Redemption! Hope! These constitute the Great Commission.

When one views the apocalyptic hope, when the lion and the lamb abide together, we do not conceive of this compatibility resulting from isolation in separate cages or restraint that may do bodily harm. Actually their compatibility is the product of voluntary behavior, an understanding of unique differences, and a respect for the rights and privileges of others. Here, precisely, is the purpose that the church must project for the ordering of lives in a world where the human factor is as diverse as that of lions and lambs in the animal kingdom.

Administrators and those responsible for administration may believe that they have little influence here. But as little as it may seem, it may multiply into every sector of life. Irregularities abound in our society, and many of them are subscribed to in the church, among them compensating for weaknesses, stretching the truth, and bending principles to support religion based on the assumption that "after all it goes for a good cause." If things cannot be fair, proper, and right in the church, where will we begin? The fiscal and administrative processes in the religious community are the place for a good beginning.

A NEW WORLD

A fifth answer to the question of the purpose of the church is a new world. Some consider the church to be a redemptive society. Its charter and mandate is to be a society intent on redeeming the world.

In periods of evangelical zeal, the church seems inspired to grow and attain such a purpose, but as the world shrinks through improved transportation and communication systems, its impact on the world and world issues seems less and less. So much so, in fact, that one of the world's greatest historians declared in the early sixties that we were at the beginning of the end of the Christian Era in human history. Considering what thirteen persons did in a primitive society and what millions of Christians should be able to do in this society, the historian's assessment of the Christian faith is a weakened position that holds little promise for the future. Christians cannot afford the luxury of indifference to this diagnosis. The church needs to redeem in time, inasmuch as one of its primary tasks is to redeem the world.

There is a new thrust toward nationalism in the world today as new nations emerge and the developing nations gain significance in the fraternity of nations. Cultures of power-lessness find a new strength, if in nothing more than the vastness of the numbers of humans they represent. Because of the numerical strength of these traditional pockets of poverty and helplessness, the nations of strength and diminishing influence are moving into a stance of isolation and self-preservation that can do little more than disrupt the peace and purity of humankind. The present trend is one of hopelessness.

Expenditure for munitions in the budgets of the nations of the world is phenomenal. Without exception, defense figures larger than any other single item of national concern. Strategic arms are developed at such a rapid pace that weapons manufactured become obsolete in a very short while. Weapons and counterweapons ensure for almost every nation the power to attack and the capability of counterattack in a limited time period. Destruction of people and property will be determined largely by who strikes first, though the world's great powers have such capability that through attacks and counterattacks there would be little to remain over which a victor might truly rejoice. Rather than victory, there is a greater likelihood of no victory at all. The world, and civilization, cannot afford the luxury of such a risk and such extravagance for a single power's gain. Survival is for all or none.

Advocacy has been one of the tools of the prophetic witness of organized religion in these times. However, the leadership of the churches, in most cases, has not communicated well with the members of the local congregations. In many cases there is as great a difference between the leaders and members of the churches as there is between church leaders and nonmembers. In this respect the church needs to define its mission, and there needs to be a concerted effort to enable church leaders and church members to come to a oneness of mind that may be communicated to the world in such a way that those outside the "society of the concerned" can become impressed with the concepts and literally connected to the process that will truly lead to a new heaven and a new earth—planets of righteousness among stars of promise and hope.

Apocalyptic hope in the Scriptures is clear: "A new heaven and a new earth wherein dwelleth righteousness." The future could provide nothing better. Humans can have no desire for anything more. Christianity proposes the implementation of this process, and the church must project the image of the evidence of the design as a primary basic purpose.

We err in assuming that ministry and mission will be in proper focus so long as the pulpit is alert to the gospel and human need; as long as the liturgy and sacraments are faithfully exercised and observed. But ministry and mission are determined by priorities, facilities, equipment, staff, and funding, and none will be orchestrated well without proper direction from the administrator and/or administrative body.

Those administrating the church's program and finances are in a unique position to focus on priorities and make certain that the ministry and mission of the church are central to all that the church and church-related agencies do.

The purposes of the church, then, are worship, prayer, witnessing, the ordering of lives, and a new world. By and large, these purposes are not known outside the circle of membership involvement, and even among those involved, there is not a clear understanding of the church's ministry and mission. These purposes must therefore be projected not only to those within the voluntary organization but to every person. No less a mandate is incorporated in the Great Commission—a commission that must bargain for nothing less.

3

Long-Range Planning
and Goal Setting

No organization suffers as much from the lack of planning as the Christian church. Most churches have all they can do to maintain their house of worship, and even in this area of responsibility, as we have seen, they are guilty of gross neglect. Much that they do is done of necessity. The search is for the most economical way to get by for the present, and there is no policy that provides funds to ensure fiscal integrity to the organization and accumulated resources to accomplish major rehabilitation and improvement at proper times.

Recently, en route to the airport in Portland, Oregon, Rodney Page, Associate Executive of Oregon Ecumenical Ministries, and I were engaged in a conversation concerning the churches. As we passed a local church, Dr. Page indicated that the particular congregation consisted of fewer than 200 members. "In fact," he said, "practically every church in the state of Oregon has fewer than two hundred members."

Can you imagine a national corporation planning stores and service units across the United States with as little planning and insight as the denominations?

Or can you imagine any corporation retaining outlets across the United States that are not productive, not meeting human needs, and not projecting an image of credibility and fiscal integrity as our denominations do? In fact, in a recent newspaper in Bergen County, New Jersey, there is the story of a closing of a Pathmark Store on Highway 17 in New Jersey, even though it occupies a comparatively new building with approximately 40,000 square feet of floor space adjacent to one of the heaviest traveled highways on the continent. Volume per square foot of space does not justify the continuation of the operation. Standing in line at the checkout counters, no one would be apt to suspect that this could indeed be a fact. But it is! The market is closing. A survey of local church worship-space needs, in the light of the sparse lines of folk entering the churches and the slender traffic in the pews, should not be nearly as difficult to calculate.

The local church is the product of little or no planning in the past or in the present, and it operates with short-term goals seldom exceeding the current budget. There is little posture suggesting direction in the future. All in all, it is a sad, sad story.

In the Great Commission there was long-range planning: to teach all nations, baptize all people. It was to encircle the human family in the love of God and bring them to a saving knowledge of the Lord and Savior, Jesus. Although the mandate is crystal clear, Christianity simply has not accepted it as its goal in long-range planning. There is no timetable. Even evangelists, whose business it is to evangelize the world, assume that there is no hope of attaining such a goal "until Jesus comes." It is time for Christianity to accept its mission seriously, enhance the Great Commission as the ultimate goal, and structure a timetable with milestones to measure progress along the way. While Jesus did not consider the ultimate goal too large for a group of thirteen persons, it seems too great for the institutional church. Remembering the ultimate goal, let us proceed to consider long-range planning at the level of the local church.

DEFINING THE PARISH

The Roman Catholic Church has traditionally defined the parish in terms of an actual geographical area. The exception has been where ministry has been to a particular language group in a particular geographical area. While Protestants have generally placed churches in convenient locations, the parish has normally been defined as those persons who, through voluntary association, have assumed membership in the local congregation. Membership is by selection—a local church selecting members, folk selecting a local church to which they will belong. The development of new members has been a primary consideration in most churches, but more recently there has been only a determination to sustain the membership at a level accepted and approved by the governing body, which consists of the officers and leaders in a local congregation. When one considers the fact that the majority of local churches in the Protestant sector consist of fewer than 200 persons, it is obvious that this is an acceptable size. Throughout the membership of the local church, there would be a denial that this is indeed the fact. They really want more people. Actually, they need more people. Few churches of 200 members or less have either the financial or personal resources to support effective ministry in any community. But members insist that they truly want to embrace the entire community. While they profess this, one knows that it is simply not true. Interpersonal relations are such that at an optimum level the forces are at work to exclude certain numbers from the inclusive fellowship of open hearts and communicating minds. More than half the people who visit a church will sense that the fellowship is closed, the welcome artificial, and the environment unfriendly to their participation in the local church.

It is important, then, that the local church define the parish. In defining the parish, the local church will be establishing a goal in terms of participation, in terms of outreach, and in terms of concern for people. Inasmuch as the

mandate of the Gospel is for every man, woman, and child—
"whosoever will, let him come,"—it is important that the
perimeter of the parish be established in terms of a reasonable, responsible, geographic area. The ultimate goal for the
local parish will be the parish lines; the lines that the parish
assumes to define its geographical area of religious concern
and obligation.

There are a number of governing factors that will define
the parish limits.

There may be natural boundaries resulting from geography and topography. These may consist of mountains and
valleys, brooks and streams, rivers and lakes, deserts and
wastelands. To a certain degree, natural limitations emerge
from the geographical and topographical factors evident
to every parish situation.

There are also community boundaries. These boundaries
are represented by railroads and factories, freeways and
thoroughfares, parks and conservation areas, schools and
shopping areas.

In addition, there are residential-type boundaries—apart-
ments, condominiums, and cooperatives; high rises and
walk-ups. There are planned communities for families and
for the aged with town houses. There are communities of
single-family dwellings. Life-styles change from one type
of residence to another, and each dimension ranges in ages,
interests, and the time that people will have for diversified
interests. In each of the residential-type situations, there
are vast differences in economic well-being. At times particular communities will span the economic spectrum.

As leaders define the parish lines, they will have to make
a determination as to whether the boundaries are insur-
mountable. Obviously the boundaries in the first category
have no flexibility, and the likelihood of reaching across
mountains, rivers, and deserts is remote. In such cases there
may be little likelihood of reaching beyond the barriers of
parks, shopping centers, and campuses. And in a given geographic location, a parish must determine whether or not it

will structure programs to reach all types of persons in different types of living quarters in those areas. Some will assume that it is more advantageous to program for a particular type. In such a case several churches may be required in a limited geographical area with each focusing on a particular type. Those who assume that a parish cannot effectively minister to all have a mind-set that simply will not enable a parish to assume a proper role with all people. This causes me to say that frequently the greatest limitations are within a given parish rather than imposed on a given parish.

In the world of business, studies are continually made to determine marketability. Changes in zoning, the demolition of properties, the erection of new structures, and significant changes in population affecting age, sex, ethnic, and racial groupings are noted carefully. Advertising, window dressing, commodity inventory, and personnel are carefully evaluated, programmed, and changed to ensure financial integrity and economic credibility.

In many instances one business closes and another takes its place. One type of operation simply is not compatible with the particular environment or the confines of the geographical area. Often profitability is the determining factor. This is not always true, however, for in many cases profitable operations have been suspended or terminated because of other factors. In one case a sizable facility was closed because the particular establishment would not be complimentary to the projected image of the corporation in other existing geographical areas and could well deter development of other outlets in new markets. Perhaps the corporation saw the handwriting on the wall. In any event it was not willing to gamble an indefinite future on a current balance sheet.

Administrators, and administration, carry the responsibility for conducting the studies and surveys that will document the projected models for ministry to be utilized by the parish for ministry and mission. Such studies and surveys should be done in concert with other denominations in order that each particular parish will complement the services and offerings of parishes in other denominations and the same care be taken in sustaining ministry and mission as is exercised through comity agreements for new church development.

DEFINING MISSION

Defining mission is a more complex process than defining a parish, since the geographical and community boundaries are quite obvious. It is not difficult to understand perimeters when they are incorporated in mountain ranges and waterways, commercial complexes and freeways, urban high rises and single-family homes. In defining mission, it is important to consider all these factors.

The usual definition of mission proceeds from certain basic assumptions. In many cases the assumptions are not valid and are based entirely on the personal attitudes and limited experience of the members of the parish. And all too often these attitudes are much too narrow in scope and simply will not stand up under careful scrutiny. We have heard folk speak of their church and say, "There are no children in the area; there are no young people in the area; there are no young adults in the area; there are no senior citizens in the area." One must not live with such assumptions until actual surveys in the community support them as factual and valid. A survey of every fifth family in the radius of a mile will provide a valid base for determining the type of folk providing potential for mission in a particular area.

In determining priority in mission, there must be a profile for the organization as well as for the community. Self-discernment, self-awareness, and self-identification are inseparable from the process of determining a church's outreach. Mission is communication, and a church cannot communicate with folk without, if there is not a compatibility of interest, type, and life within. A local church cannot determine where it is going if it does not know where it is.

The administrator, and administration, is in a unique position to guide leadership through the process of developing the profiles in the parish and in the community and to assist the program departments in defining mission for effective and meaningful ministry. Frequently there will be a void in the parish of those types of persons required for ministry and mission to groups identified in the community. Here the more difficult task in evangelism emerges, as there is the need to develop from outside the parish the core group that will become the instrumentality for meaningful mission in both the parish and community.

Business has the advantage of advertising, introductory offers, coupons, bonuses, and free samples. In spite of the fact that the church is not a business enterprise, it does have much to sell. And it may well advertise its "product," make known unusual "benefits," and give witness to "satisfied customers."

Perhaps a grave error in the church is a tendency to impress folk with "what we are doing" rather than with "what you could be doing" with our church. Advertisers want to put you in the driver's seat, before the twenty-five-inch picture tube, at the end of the new golf club, and in a smartly tailored fur coat. The products are not for others—the products are for you! The focus is on the prospect. The purpose: to get each individual involved.

The task in religion is similar.

Having identified types and discovered core groups or instrumentalities both within and without the congregation, the church can begin to define its mission—and a mission defined is a mission well on the way to fulfillment.

DETERMINING NEED

The world is in need of redemption, and since the geographical area in which we minister is a part of the world, it is a part of the world that needs redemption. In the

church we need to address ourselves to the various redemptive processes that are required in the community and
to the redemptive processes that we, as a church, may be
instrumental in effecting. The Great Commission requires
that we teach all nations and baptize all people. The intent
of that instruction and the intent of that baptism is subject
to debate and speculation. In my reading of the Gospels, I
have become convinced that the Great Commission requires
that we address all areas of need and include the entire
human family in the redemptive process. There is no healing
initiative that is outside the church's province.

Recently I was consulting with the Board of Directors
for United Ministries for Higher Education in New York
State in a meeting in Buffalo. In the course of the day, the
board was urged to consider the need for the vocational
guidance of students majoring in special fields where the
supply exceeded the demand. Since Watergate, investigative
reporting has been a popular major in the schools of journal-
ism. There is presently a larger enrollment in our colleges
and universities majoring in this area than there are positions
in newspapers across the United States. Three out of four
of these persons will not be able to exercise their expertise
in the area of their professional proficiency. Determining
a strategy in counseling and alternate vocational choices
was considered a missionary enterprise for the group. Our
Lord requires that we provide an alternate calling. This is
a part of the missionary enterprise. Now one might say that
there are so few persons in a single parish for whom this
would be a problem that it would be ridiculous to include
this as an aspect of mission. In many parishes this would be
true. However, in every geographical area, at any particular time, there are those who are changing vocations,
and some of them are in need of a new direction in their
lives. The church should be an instrument to their peace in
this difficult period.

While it is impossible to structure programs to meet
each particular need in a group setting, it is not impossible

to structure counseling opportunities and services that may meet individual needs. I have never ceased to be impressed by the fact that each Sunday the program at the Fifth Avenue Presbyterian Church in New York City carries the announcement: EMPLOYMENT ADVICE AVAILABLE IN THE VESTRY AFTER THE MORNING SERVICE. This is an administrative detail but certainly an offering that is at the very heart of the Gospel.

Move from this illustration for the parish community and you will discover literally hundreds of needs that are a part of the redemptive process and inseparable from Christian mission.

Having engaged in the survey process in which we identify various concerns, we are in a position to define needs, and those involving the greatest number of persons in all likelihood will result in identifying them as basic priorities. There will be those that will affect thousands of people, those that will affect hundreds of people, and those that will affect dozens of people. And there will be those that affect a single person. The larger the group need, the greater the urgency to respond in affirmative action for mission. And the urgency of a single situation may result in a priority consideration as well.

DETERMINING CAPABILITY

Having determined the need, there is the task of determining the capability of the particular church or organization to respond to basic needs as defined in the community profile.

A process within the local church similar to the process in the community will provide a profile of the local congregation and reveal the potential within the parish for developing a program to meet the basic needs in the community. It may be that the priorities that exist in the community as determined by the profile in needs will not match the profile in the congregation for the greater potential in responding to, or meeting, those needs. In each case, however, the parish should design the program to capitalize on its greater capabilities with a determination to develop a greater constituency to meet the community needs in total as time goes on.

There is much disappointment in church programs because many of the programs announced and planned simply do not address the needs of either the parish or the community. Many of the programs planned by the church are based on an earlier period of our nation's history and do not take into account the societal changes that have caused many program offerings to become obsolete. In some cases they are not obsolete because of programming as much as because of timing. Much of the local church's programming is still scheduled for Sunday. Sunday is no longer exclusively the Lord's Day, and changes in life-styles and time prioritizing make it impractical for the church to do extensive programming in this way.

Look at our present calendar. Two Sundays each year are limited in participation by Daylight Saving Time. Five weekends each year are scheduled as three-day weekends. Often in the public schools, teachers' institutes are on Fridays, providing one or two additional three-day weekends for folk with young children. In 1977 and 1978 both Christmas and New Year's made two additional three-day weekends. (These holidays are three-day weekends about half the time.) Studies of weather trends indicate that there is an average of five Sundays each year adversely affected by weather conditions. This means that the Sunday program of the church is in jeopardy approximately 25 percent of the time. Can you imagine any other enterprise programmed with as many limitations and risks as the Sunday/weekend offerings of the church?

In programming the local church's effort, it is important that community needs be known, internal program capabilities determined, objectives defined, and the weekly/monthly/quarterly and annual schedules established to maximize the organization's effectiveness.

Having done this, a goal-setting process should be implemented with a definition of primary, secondary, tertiary, and ultimate goals.

The primary goal will be the immediate objective within an organization's reach, taking into consideration limitations of time and the availability of personnel and resources. It should be attainable in a comparatively limited period of time and should move the organization in a direction to generate enthusiasm and a sense of attainment, which will boost morale in the organization and confirm integrity in the institution.

In the world of business, it may be a Fall Sale, Anniversary Event, Spring Festival. There is a time frame, a volume figure, and a dollar value. The total organization moves in concert toward the objective and there is much enthusiasm as the goal is attained.

The religious calendar and a particular organization's track record provide a wealth of opportunity for each local church.

The secondary goal will be a point of accomplishment consistent with the primary goal and clearly defined in the organization's purpose in ministry and mission. The secondary goal will be a significant part of the total purpose as defined in perhaps a more limited area of the organization's life.

In the world of business, it may be a departmental thrust uniquely relating to the primary goal in which there is a happy marriage between the objective and the potential and capability of a particular departmental offering.

The organizational and departmental structures within a religious organization make possible unique opportunities to assist the institution in the attainment of the primary goal.

The tertiary goal will be a point of accomplishment consistent with the secondary goal, supportive of the primary goal, and clearly defined in the organization's purpose in ministry and mission. The tertiary goal will be a significant part of the secondary goal as defined in perhaps an even more limited area of the organization's life.

In business the primary goal may be an anniversary sale, a secondary goal the special offerings of the radio and television departments, and the tertiary goal a volume thrust in citizens band radios consisting of a quality product at a rock-bottom price.

It does not take much imagination in the local church and religious establishment to discover those entities that may uniquely strengthen the secondary goal and provide substantial support to the primary goal in a limited time span.

The ultimate goal, of course, is contained in the teachings of Jesus and included in the Great Commission. Each institution will need to define what that means for them. The ultimate goal is a shared goal, and each local church and agency contributes to the attainment of that ultimate goal by preparing leaders, enlightening constituency, and developing financial support in those areas in which it works, as well as in those areas for which it has delegated responsibility for ministry and mission beyond the immediate geographical area of the parish's life and work.

Long-range planning and goal setting will not become a fact if they are not implemented through the administrator and/or administration. They do not happen by themselves. They require the defining of the parish; outlining of mission; determination of need; discernment of capability; and crystal-clear articulation of primary, secondary, and tertiary goals. Without them the church can neither honor its purpose nor attain its objective.

4

The Roles of Drivers
and Dissenters in the
Administrative Process

With eight fingers and two thumbs, children of nursery age are taught the rhyme, "This is the church and this is the steeple, Open the door and here are the people."

It is not until we open the door that we come to the real church. The church is people. The body of Christ. The sheep in the pasture. A personal, political entity.

Wherever you find people, you find leaders and followers. You find those with a sense of direction and you find those seeking direction. You find those who contest for a greater influence and you find those who rally to the support of one or another because a meeting of minds or a warmth of heart causes them to believe that one is a better way. As the struggle becomes more intense among those exercising influence, it becomes more complex among those seeking direction. Where opposing forces become intense, a moderate position emerges that either becomes the prominent position or erodes a single position to the extent that the other becomes the prominent position. At times the weakened group will become the loyal opposition or dissociate from the organization to form a new group. The moderate group usually remains a part of the original organizational structure. In each segment of these classifications, there are drivers and there are dissenters. Drivers are those persons that enable a group to sustain direction and accomplish purpose. Dissenters are those who disturb the peace and tranquility of the organization.

In a group as small as two persons you have a leader and a follower. Unless one is a leader and one a follower, it will never be a group. In a group as small as three persons you have a leader, a follower, and a dissenter. Multiply the numbers to any size and all three components will be present. The leadership group will be the smallest. The followers' group will be the largest and the dissenting, or differing, group of significant proportion. But throughout the course of the organizational life, there will be varying intensities in all segments. Leaders will lead with more or less enthusiasm. Followers will follow with more or less interest. Moderates will become involved in a greater or lesser degree. Life is not static and organizational structures are not concrete.

Organizations go through cycles, just as individuals do, and these vary from one extreme to the other. At times all will go well. Leadership is good and projects firm objectives. At times the objectives are not firm and in some cases are unacceptable to many, either because they do not understand the goals or do not concur with the goals in focus at the time. This makes for schism (i.e., objectives focusing on differing goals). Followers become confused and ultimately align their support and influence on one or another. In some cases there will be a negotiating process wherein forces unite, compromises are made, and new objectives and goals emerge as the fellowship continues with vigor and strength. In some cases negotiation is out of the question. Leaders will not lead. Objectives and goals have been fixed. There is a determination to proceed regardless of all others. Groupings emerge in support or in dissension. In many cases the mind-sets are fixed to the degree that the closest thing to compromise is a willingness to separate into two or more groups or organizations.

In all these processes there are two important types: the drivers and the dissenters. Let us consider them one at a time.

DRIVERS

The drivers are those who are capable of enabling an organization to proceed and progress in a defined pattern. While they are not infallible (and in some cases the results of their efforts will be undesirable, disappointing, and unsatisfactory), they do, nevertheless, enable an organization to move from one place to another. Goals, or countergoals resulting from missing the mark, are the milestones of their progressiveness.

In this area many leaders who, in a real sense of the word, are drivers are led astray by the assumption that drivers are always drivers and that drivers are always capable of driving regardless of the course or objective. In no other place in the world is this as obvious as in the church and in pastoral ministry. A pastor assumes a position, takes inventory of the leadership potential in a congregation, discovers those whom he or she can trust and who seem trustworthy and trusting of him or her, and proceeds to launch a program through the several stages of ministry. This program may span five or ten years; sometimes a lifetime. Some of the programs go very well. Some do not go at all. They do not go at all simply because the clergyperson presumes that folk who are drivers in one area will be drivers in all areas and that they are capable of bringing each and every program to a successful conclusion. Most do not realize that every cause, every objective, every goal, and every purpose will gain its strength, rally support, and proceed best with a constituency all its own.

The world of business has discovered this, and great effort is made to discover the constituency that will be responsible for each new product, new facility, or new corporate structure. Unless there is a constituency of strength, and evidence of significant leadership within, the risk of introduction, expansion, or restructure is never undertaken.

The fact that all cannot be effective in all things is obvious in certain of the programs in the local church. One group will do fabulously well with children, another with young people, another with young adults, another with adults, and still another with the aged. However, take any of those groupings and you will discover that there are vast differences among the leaders in any particular age group. Some may be drivers in sports and recreation. Some may be drivers in science and industry. Some may be drivers in religion and the arts. Because one is a driver in sports does not mean that that person will be a driver in the arts. Because one is a driver in religion does not mean that that person will be a driver in science. Because one is a driver in industry does not mean that that one will be a driver in recreation. The sooner we realize this in leadership roles, the more successful we are likely to be in effecting results from and through local leaders.

The primary task in proceeding with drivers is the task of understanding issues and determining the groupings of folk relating to particular issues. All of us at one time or another have been assumed by someone to be drivers, and an assumption has been made that we will exercise leadership in a particular area. How uncomfortable we become when it is obvious that our interest has been misread and misunderstood. In fact, the leader loses credibility and those assumed to be drivers tend to become less enthusiastic even in the areas of their most vital interests simply because they feel that they have been taken and that an effort has been made to coerce them in a direction in which they simply are not interested in going.

The matching of drivers to causes in which they are interested, have capability, and will exercise their talent is of primary importance in organizational development. It is expedient that the leadership in the local parish take full inventory of the program needs in the community and match the potential of those capable of moving the organization to a responsive and responsible position in bridging the opportunities evident in the community with the mission for which the parish has been organized.

The process of timing is as important as the process of matching program potential with the talent of those who are the drivers. Here there is a need for leaders to understand the ability of those who are the drivers to effect the change necessary to bring a project to completion. If the movement is too soon, or too late, the project simply does not materialize. Many achieving stature in leadership roles do so not because they excel as leaders as such, but simply because the program to which they relate has been timed, or occurred, at the right time for maximum results.

I think back through the years of the automotive industry and remember how the Ford Motor Company moved from the Model T to the Model A and on to the V-8. Each was a significant change and timed to consumer acceptance. Those were the days of the Austin as well. Compact. Economical. Easy to handle. But the time simply was not ripe. It was not ripe in the United States or anyplace else in the world. Every study produced evidence that the time was not ripe. The manufacturer believed that folk would change their minds once the product was available. The manufacturer was right, but the product could not wait fifty years for public acceptance. And the Austin has gone the way of the LaSalle, the Studebaker, and the Kaiser.

Timing may be both coincidental and providential. Certainly some in history have attained greatness simply because they were at the right place at the right time. Circumstances resulted in a constituency response to a need, and as leadership emerged they responded to the situation as imperative to their future. Many in a leadership role would have experienced the same success.

Certainly at times timing seems to be providential. A cause has emerged over a period of time and came to a moment of consummation as though it were God-given.

A leader, too, almost out of the blue, emerges as though he or she were the answer to prayer. A constituency is ready to act. God appears to be fulfilling his mission in time. Leaders, followers, and dissenters move in a steady manner. There is little or no schism, distress, or concern over the course of events. The program progresses harmoniously and successfully. There is little doubt in anyone's mind but that this is the will of God.

Through the marriage of time and need, and the concerted effort of leaders, followers, and dissenters, programs are able to move and organizational progress is firm and good.

Proper timing means that the time is right in terms of a favorable environment. It also means that the time is right in terms of the availability of resources. The best of causes at a most appropriate time simply cannot come to full fruition if there is an absence of resources to make the program possible. Resources may not be natural, manufactured, or monetary. Usually the material and manufactured resources may be made possible if there is adequate financing, even when the project/program is not in the proximity of the natural and/or manufactured resources. Transportation and communication can minimize complications evident when location is not actually opportune. Adequate financial resources can often bring many problems to solution even when components are not conducive to fulfillment. With adequate resources the leaders may lead, drivers may drive, and followers may follow to maximum advantage.

DISSENTERS

A second group evident in the scene of events is the dissenters. While providing evidence of activity, it is not always with direction and most often not programmed toward the goals of the church, agency, or group. Let us consider them now.

As drivers they are vocal, but their voice is in opposition, raising doubts and usually without positive direction.

They raise questions: What? When? Where? Why? For whom? The answers are not of primary importance. The questions are raised simply because there will not be one answer but many answers, inasmuch as the questions will not be directed to a single individual but will be raised in a group; at times there will be as many answers as there are people hearing the questions. The more numerous the answers, the more satisfying the process for those dissenting, for their intent is not unity but disunity, not consensus but diversity, not a singleness of mind but a confusion of thought. When there is diversity, disunity, and confusion, the dissenter has accomplished his or her purpose. Progress has been impeded, and that is the dissenter's objective.

Dissenters express doubts. For every success story in the biographical history of people and nations, there are dozens of accounts of failure. The lure to success lies in the fact that it is the exception to the rule. The rule ought to be plain and simple good fortune. We did it, we achieved it, we gained it. The dissenter will remind you that for every one who did it, there were a dozen that could not do it; for every one who did achieve, a hundred failed; and for every one who gained the desired goal, there were a thousand who could never become "king of the hill." The emphasis on the nonachievers and underachievers becomes paramount, and through it the dissenter has attained his or her purpose.

Dissenters make articulate their fears. These fears are not always theirs, nor are they necessarily the express fears from their life and experience, but they are graphic enough to find a resting place in cautious minds present in every group. For some it is the fear of the new. For some, the fear of the old. For some, the fear of the untried or untested. For some, the fear of the result that simply cannot be known unless tried. But the dissenters have given birth to fear, and through it they have attained their purpose.

Dissenters vocalize the irrelevant. There are few delaying

tactics so effective as muddying the waters in an issue-oriented meeting. The remote as well as the absurd become matters of interest and concern, since at least a few in every group attune their interest and concern to that which is irrelevant. Because of this, the interest of the group loses focus and becomes diversified, and the dissenters have attained their purpose.

Leaders must identify the dissenters and take measures to direct their questions to refining the decision-making process in order that they appear to be supportive rather than divisive. Couching them in proper terms and settings, one may eliminate doubts, remove fears, and set aside the irrelevant. Rumor and falsehood can be identified for what they really are.

Objectives can be reached through the concerted efforts of those who drive in spite of the object or course developed by dissenters who would disrupt the process and stimulate confusion and doubt.

Dissenters ought to be defined and understood as members of a loyal opposition and credibility assigned to their procedures toward refining the decision-making processes of the group.

Drivers provide direction and enable leaders to attain their desired goal, and they are delightful. Dissenters are seldom appreciated. When reviewing the course of events, however, it is likely that progress is more sure and the ultimate goal of greater worth as a result of the testing and refining that has occurred because of the dissenters' negative input along the way.

Administrators and administration can do much in guiding the selection process for enrolling drivers who can deal with particular issues and programs and who can test the validity of dissenting influences that seem to impede progress in order that the organization may be strengthened as a result of it. Continually the administrators must monitor the processes that will bring the organization to proper objectives.

5

Funding Mission

I have often said that I am a "marrying parson." But after saying this, I hasten to admit that I have been a better burying parson than a marrying parson. Everyone that I have buried is still buried, but everyone that I have married is not still married. I am a marrying parson and my task is to marry resources to need. There is nothing in the world that cannot be funded. The difficulty is in bringing together those things that need to be funded with the resources that will be available to fund them.

When we talk about marriage, there are some who say, "But many persons never marry." I have seldom met a person who could say that he or she has never had an opportunity for marriage. Usually the opportunity is not advantaged as in the case of the single lady who said, "Yes, there was Sam, but who would ever have married Sam?" At times the very source that would have funded a program has been passed over because those responsible for the funding did not take the opportunity seriously.

Funding mission requires the utilization of a formula provided by Jesus of Nazareth in the Gospels: "Ask, and ye shall receive; seek, and ye shall find; knock, and it shall be opened unto you." While this is the formula for funding mission, and there are no substitutes, a great deal of attention must go into packaging the need and considering likely sources for funding.

PACKAGING THE NEED

Planners are important to the process inasmuch as there cannot be funding without planning. When one considers planning as a part of the process that defines the need, there is no question concerning the validity of that assumption. Here is one of the biggest areas of weakness in the funding processes for most organizations today. There are four clear guidelines in packaging needs.

1. A funding need must be defined in such a way that it can be clearly discerned as a significant and vital part of the organization's life and/or mission. Most of our funding needs are defined in general terms and are treated with the same respect and understanding of general funds and do not generate enthusiasm or command much support. But when clearly defined in terms of significance and worth, a need will attract attention among those who have the wherewithal to fund it.

2. A funding need must be attractively packaged. In this, organizational planners have much to learn from the commercial enterprises of our time.

We are participants in a society in which the packaging of foods, commodities, and materials is of great importance. Items will not sell unless they are attractively packaged. Often more skill is required in preparing the package than in preparing the product itself. As a result, our bulk of disposable items often is greater than the bulk of our purchased commodities. This, in time, will change. But until it does, those in marketing will continue to emphasize the significance and importance of packaging products. Funding requires that we package the need in significant and inviting wrappings.

Much of our church-related funding needs come up short simply because we do not couch them in the setting they require to challenge the adequate support to which they are entitled.

3. A funding need must be reasonably and properly sized. Here in the area of religion, we have much to learn from the marketplace. In religion the common assumption is that a single size will accommodate all funding sources.

In the dry-goods store every item of clothing is sized to fit persons of various heights and weights. The closest you can come to a general size category is small, medium, large, and extra large. And those four classifications are not sufficient for all items. In shoe sizes there will be a size 10 and even that will be subdivided into an A, AA, AAA, AAAA, B, C, D, E, EE, EEE, and EEEE.

In the grocery store there are few items that are not available in more than one quantity of packaging. Canned goods come in several sizes. Frozen foods are packaged in various quantities. Wrapped meats are marketed with numerous weights.

In the automobile showrooms there are several models of the same type of car, but the number of cylinders varies from car to car, the horsepower varies from motor to motor, and the size of the body varies from auto to auto. Some folk will require a coupe and others a station wagon. Some will prefer eight cylinders and others four or six. Some will prefer a car with a lot of leg room and trunk space and others will be content with very little. The American people would never have emerged as two- and three-car families if every automobile were of the same size and style.

Consider the funding needs in the church and church-related organizations. Usually they are defined in general terms and the entire funding need is described in such terms that it is to be considered by the entire body of individuals and the funding need met by a combined response. The entire funding need is seldom presented to a single individual. Single individuals are presented the entire package and, if they are to consider it in terms of their own financial capability, they are required to apply a mathematical formula that emerges from their own experience or the numbers game in which they divide the funding need by the membership in the organization to determine their "fair share."

A fair share is never a proper share. Proper shares may vary with individuals in terms of interest, priorities, involvement, and concern. A fair share will result in an astronomical figure for several for whom the program or project has little or no significant worth. A fair share will result in a far too modest sum for those for whom the project or program has a great significance.

Funding needs must be sized to accommodate the economic and interest potential of individuals and/or families related to the organization's life and work.

The economic and interest level varies from individual to individual and from giving unit to giving unit. However, in the religious society we tend to err by modifying our financial askings to a level commensurate with the funding support level of the average person or giving unit. There is no such thing as an average person! There is no average giving unit!

A funding need may be larger than any individual and larger than a composite of the average calculated for a member/giving constituency. But the funding need may be sized into various components in which certain descriptive portions will exceed the average calculated gift potential and certain others will be more modest than the average gift potential.

4. Each funding need must be a part of the whole. In packaging needs or program opportunities, it is important that each be defined and constitute a project unto itself. A sound basis of operation is to define and price the funding need in such a way that if it is the only item funded, it is a project that can stand on its own two feet whether any or all other funding needs are met. Usually this can be done.

At times the overall plan will be changed to accommodate a funding opportunity that merely funds a piece of the action.

Many funding needs are not met because they are not departmentalized and opportunity is not provided to sources of lesser means to fund portions of the overall program. Also, many funding needs are not met because the total funding need is beyond the realm of possibility from a single source and the various components are not structured to accommodate the whole.

Four things are important to remember in this area of development: First, define the need clearly. Second, package the need attractively. Third, price the opportunity reasonably and properly. Fourth, orchestrate the funding opportunities to support the total program.

Once the need has been defined and the proposals packaged and priced, it is important to consider the funding sources.

CONSIDERING THE SOURCES

There are five significant funding sources in our society today: individuals, foundations, corporations, organizations, and government.

Individuals. We consider our society a free society, and an important part of that free society is voluntary organizations. People are free to select the organizations to which they will belong and, inasmuch as participation is voluntary, they can, within the limits of the organization itself, move in and out of membership as they choose. And within these same limits they may determine the measure of financial support they will provide to the organization as well.

Persons with significant resources are important in meeting the funding needs in organizations. Usually in major campaigns 60 percent of the funding will come from 10 percent of the organization's membership. Fund raisers are certain to say, "If you want money, you must go where the money is." Statistical data confirms this thesis. The most generous segment in our society from a percentage point of view is the group whose taxable income exceeds $100,000 per year.

Persons of modest means are equally important. Each of those holding membership in the organization is important. "Everyone needs to participate in the effort to meet the funding need." This, too, is an important rule of funds development people. And the fact that those who have taxable incomes of less than $5000 per year are the second most generous persons in our society today, on a percentage basis, supports that thesis.

But there are many sources among individuals that are exceptional to those two groups. At the level of a local church, as an example, there is one among each forty persons who is capable of giving as much as the other thirty-nine persons together, if so motivated. These may not be among those whose income is less than $5000 or more than $100,000 a year.

The most modest contributions are those from folk whose taxable incomes are between $15,000 and $30,000 per year. Many times we consider these folk on their way up, folk who are overextending themselves, and folk for whom primary interests relate to business rather than to voluntary organizations. This may or may not be true. To assume that it is true, or always true, is a gross mistake. Because of limited performance they are the most neglected group, and the group of greatest potential for support, in our society today.

In this respect we need to determine where they are and where their greater interests lie. Here is the one area where we suffer the most because of our traditional funding processes.

To what causes do people lend their financial support?

What approach was made to solicit their gift?

How large was the gift?

How was the gift programmed? Weekly? Monthly?

Quarterly? Semiannually? Annually? Other?

What was the duration of the fund commitment period?

What were the designations?

How was the pay-up?

In most cases such records are discarded when the pay-up period has expired. And in most cases, records dealing with the financial development processes are destroyed just as soon as the campaign is completed and before the participants are a great distance into the pay-up period.

Each time we enter into a financial campaign in a local church or agency, we begin from scratch. We do not have a track record of support, interests, special concerns, or special gifts unless they are of an unusual or major type. Only in the cases where the gifts are substantial and permanently identified do we have a basis for askings and support.

Look over the history of your organization. What details do you have from the last annual campaign? What details are available from previous campaigns? What experience is available from the capital funds efforts that have been programmed in previous years? What learnings can we gain from the past?

In the economic order each new venture begins with a comprehensive review of corporate experience in the field. For new corporations it is a study of experience and track record in like situations. Decisions, wherever possible, are made on proven experience.

We need to look, too, to the experience of other organizations in the particular community and area. Some will number members of your constituency among them. Learnings from their experience will be supportive of your processes.

Many times it is a person with a widow's mite, or a person whom one would not assume to have interest or funding capability, who comes through with the most significant gifts. And without a previous track record we have no idea who or where these persons are.

In this respect we need to be mindful of timing as well.

Past giving records provide a key to the season when a person can most readily respond to a funding need. We must keep this fact uppermost in our minds. The person who has contributed in March may well respond most favorably to our appeal in that season of the year. The fact that he or she has given at that time indicates that it was a favorable season for that individual then. Follow the clues from that experience in terms of date, amount, description or designation, and commitment, and you will have a solid base upon which to build continuing and expanding support.

Everyone has a right to share—those who can give substantial sums as well as those who can give modest amounts, those who will respond with a one-time gift and those who can program their giving over a period of time (for example, one, three, or five years). Personally, I have had great success with the ten-quarter model.

Serious consideration needs to be given to automatic funds transfers and adequate opportunity for those who would program gifts, either one time or at regular intervals, through their bank-card accounts. The population of the United States is approximately 217 million people. As of December 1978 there were over 575 million multiple-use cards (BankAmericard/Visa, Master Charge, American Express, Diners Club, Carte Blanche, etc.) among American consumers. Some have cried an alarm inasmuch as personal indebtedness in the United States has reached an all-time high. Their concerns are not well grounded until they compute the plastic currency factor in which considerable funding is processed within a thirty-day period.

The Counselor Association, Inc., introduced bank-card opportunities for purchasing resources in financial development to the religious constituency in 1974. Volume increased by 30 percent. In the first year, one in ten transactions involved plastic currency. In less than five years, it has moved from one in ten to more than one in three. The volume of dollars is of even greater significance.

Plastic currency is the money market of the future, and organized religion needs to recognize this fact and accommodate processes that are accepted patterns in the economic life of people today. Electronic processes that program support from individual checking accounts to organizational accounts are of great importance in keeping support at a constant level, and regularity eliminates the risk of weather, illness, and/or inconvenience.

All these opportunities must be available to individuals if maximum resources are to be provided from this sector of the philanthropic scene.

Foundations. Many individuals, families, corporations, and organizations have established foundations as an instrument for funding the philanthropic enterprise in which they may have an interest or may be capable of extending their goals. There are more than 20,000 foundations in the United States, and in our world of cosmopolitan living, their number is increasing in all sections of the free world.

The same kinds of information we found to be significant concerning individuals—their interest, patterns for giving, and the timing of their gifts—are likewise important keys to funding by foundations. To this end there are several handbooks that are helpful.

THE FOUNDATION DIRECTORY. The Foundation Directory is published every several years by the Columbia University Press. The most recent edition was published in 1977 and sold for $37.50. In it, by state in an alphabetical listing, are the foundations in the United States with assets of a million dollars or more. For each foundation there is included the full name and address of the foundation, the executive director, the trustees, and the declared purposes of the foundation, together with information concerning capital funds, sums distributed in a single year, and the number of grants, as well as the amounts of the largest and the smallest grants.

THE GRANTS INDEX. The Grants Index is published by Columbia University Press annually and provides a listing of grants announced by foundations in the United States to various agencies. Each grant is identified by a number, and information is provided concerning the size of the grant, the name of the agency receiving the grant, and the purpose for which the grant was made. A comprehensive index provides easy reference to subject matter for grants and provides opportunity for people to determine those sources that may be likely to have an interest in their project. One must remember that the Grants Index contains only those grants which a particular foundation chooses to announce in this manner to the general public.

THE NATIONAL CONSULTATION ON FINANCIAL DEVELOPMENT. This nonprofit agency, a division of The Counselor Association, Inc., with offices at 31 Langerfeld Road in Hillsdale, New Jersey 07642, and the Interchurch Center in New York City, is organized to serve the nonprofit sector and specializes in services to denominations, judicatories, local churches, and their related agencies. It provides three unique services in the foundation field:

1. NCFD will write a proposal. The fee in 1979 was $115 unless exceptional time and expertise were required and additional cost incurred. In these events the fee is adjusted to the cost required for the process.
2. NCFD will conduct a funding search and provide to an agency the ten most likely funding sources for funding a particular proposal. It does not require that it be retained to prepare the proposal for this service. Information provided on each funding source will include a track record of funding experience similar to the funding need. The cost for this service in 1979 was $85.
3. Twice each year, in October and March, NCFD submits proposals in synopsis form to 500 foundations. A proposal must be limited to one side of a single sheet of stationery, in a format consistent with the model on page 82 of *New Models for Financing the Local Church* (Raymond B. Knudsen, Association

Press, 1974). The price for this service in 1979 was $70. Three out of ten proposals submitted through this process have received some funding. NCFD adjusts its fee schedule to the inflationary index annually.

STATE FOUNDATION DIRECTORIES. Each agency should have available directories of the foundations within its geographical area. These are usually available from the state and/or city public library. Sometimes they are published by the state printing office and sometimes by agencies chartered within the state.

OTHER FOUNDATION MATERIALS. A number of additional materials are available from other sources. Most of them are quite costly and it is not practical for many of the smaller agencies to invest in them when contracted services in financial development may be secured for a rather modest fee on a per diem or piecework basis.

There are seven significant keys to the funds-development process for foundation funding.

1. The proposal should be brief, limited to not more than three pages.

2. The proposal should provide a good description of the project.

3. The proposal should describe the project in ecumenical and nonsectarian terms.

4. The proposal should include a time schedule that will not begin for at least six months from the date the proposal is submitted for funding. (Twelve or eighteen months is even better.)

5. The proposal should include a budget wherein the funding need is less than the cost of the project.

6. The proposal should provide evidence of the financial support of other funding sources.

7. The proposal should provide evidence that the project can be completed through the foundation's funding or evidence that the program may be funded by other sources at the completion of the grant period.

Corporations. Corporate support is closely related to foundation funding, but the funding is directly from the corporation and its earnings or capital and not from funds placed in a related corporation called a foundation. Gifts or grants from corporations are usually less significant in size for many reasons, among which these are the most important:

1. Corporations are not formed to give money away. They are formed to make money. Many give away less than 2 percent of their profits.

2. Corporations usually make contributions in the geographical areas where they have plants or outlets. The appeals for funding are legion. In most cases corporations prefer to give a little to many causes rather than larger amounts to few causes.

3. Intelligent philanthropy takes time, and most corporations do not provide adequate time to analyze requests or proposals, visit agencies seeking support, or monitor the project or program when funded.

One can never be sure whether a corporation has a foundation or not. Some do. Most do not. International Business Machines Corporation, as an example, does not have a foundation. The Shell companies do. In this respect the Foundation Directory and such publications as Standard & Poor's complement each other.

Corporate support can be sizable and significant in funding projects and programs. Some helpful suggestions may make for significant support.

1. Invite financial support from the large corporations having plants, warehouses, distributorships, and outlets in your geographical area. Support from the smaller corporations will come from those in your immediate area.

2. Make known your needs for gifts in kind. Equipment, supplies, materials, and services will often be more readily available to organizations and institutions than financing will. Surplus and obsolescent items are of great value to

the nonprofit institution/organization. One corporation provided the graphic arts services for an organization's annual fund drive. Another corporation provided a bus for transporting participants to a significant event. A third corporation assigned an executive vice-president to resolve a managerial problem in an agency. Needs must be requisitioned by an agency, publicized by the organization, and identified as projects to which corporations may relate.

3. Identify needs to which a corporation may relate. Many feel it important to be known for their community service, and various things in your organization will enhance the corporate image by virtue of the fact that the enterprise may be seen, and sometimes heard, through markers, printed pages, announcements, and tributes. While some will seek anonymity, many will prefer that their gift be recognized loudly and clearly.

In terms of percentage of all funding, corporation support is modest. But it can become truly significant when solicited in meaningful and responsible ways.

Organizations. Often we consider organizations at the receiving end of the philanthropic process rather than at the benevolent end. But remember that many organizations in our society generate funds for the sole purpose of giving their money away. This is illustrated by a missionary society in a local church. Journey up and down the thoroughfares of the voluntary society and you will find organizations sharing generously with other organizations as their priorities are met, concerns advanced, and dedication to human needs understood.

Consider the various types of organizations included in the philanthropic process.

NATIONAL ORGANIZATIONS. These organizations have chapters or units throughout the country and receive support not only through philanthropic processes but through memberships in chapters and/or units. Among their priorities often are the funding of experimental and demonstration programs, the development of a new or unusual service, and the strengthening of an area presently weak in the organizational process.

REGIONAL AND LOCAL ORGANIZATIONS. These organizations have causes that arise out of the geographical areas and depend upon other organizations to carry out functions that they are unable to do themselves. At times these procedures are followed in order that one organization attain its purpose more economically and efficiently.

FRATERNAL AND SOCIAL ORGANIZATIONS. Many of these membership-type organizations depend upon the program organizations to provide services that they are willing to fund but are not organized or chartered to do themselves. Their gifts, often modest in size, tend to provide special equipment and sometimes the regular undesignated general funding so necessary to agencies requiring funding for their core budget through annual contributions.

SERVICE CLUBS. These are sometimes referred to as luncheon clubs. They are organized primarily to provide social opportunities for members, and their social aspect is enhanced through projects generating funds to distribute annually as charitable contributions. Usually these organizations have preferences for funding services to the disadvantaged, and their gifts provide opportunity for the organization to be recognized for its philanthropic deeds. Those seeking funding from them will do well to arrange for significant publicity at the time the gift is made.

CHURCH GROUPS. Much of the significant philanthropic work in the world today receives little publicity or recognition because the support means is carried on through the service and concern of organizations, societies, and clubs within local churches. Hardly a group is not engaged in a decision-making process as to what support it will provide to meet a particular need in every business session. There are sometimes programs sponsored by the denomination, ecumenical organizations, other groups within the local church, and causes requiring support in areas of social concern and human need. Many in development overlook the readiness of such groups to respond generously to their support.

Organizations provide a significant funding in our society today, and the value of philanthropic dollars is increased considerably through movement of funds from one agency to another in carrying out their mission.

Government. Many Americans were surprised when the Filer Report disclosed that the flow of grant funding through the nonprofit sector almost matches dollar for dollar the generosity of the American people in both current and deferred support. In 1975 the American people provided approximately $25 billion for the support of nonprofit agencies. The federal government's expenditure totaled $23.5 billion through many of these organizations. It is interesting to note that the governmental sector considers voluntary support appropriate to public sharing as well as private sharing.

A helpful publication from the United States Printing Office is the Catalogue of Federal Domestic Assistance, which is published annually with three quarterly supplements. It includes information concerning each agency in government providing grants, the purpose of the agency, its budget, the average size of its grants, and the types of agencies that qualify for funding. Those seeking funding for mission will want to look for the words "nonprofit corporation."

In seeking funding from the federal government for churches and church-related programs, it is sometimes expedient for the agency to establish a separate nonprofit corporate structure to carry out its objectives through a grant-funded enterprise. These enterprises, of course, must be defined as nonsectarian, multiracial, and multiethnic.

Grantsmanship of this type is not only an evidence of faith and goodwill in the voluntary system but also a confirmation of the fact that government depends on people and agencies to carry out legislated programs. If the nonprofit agencies were to discontinue many of their services, it would be necessary for government to assume responsibility for them, and in most cases they would be more costly, less efficient, and less effective.

We are too close to the results of Proposition 13 in California to assess its effect. Frankly, I believe that the result in the reduction of tax dollars will make for fewer governmental services and fewer grants to the voluntary agencies. A significant increase in the need for agency responsibility in areas abdicated by government will result in the need for more philanthropic dollars from individuals and a more effective delivery system of services through the nonprofit sector.

Funding by government to the nonprofit sector is available not only from the federal government but from state and municipal governments as well. At times this type of funding is on a matching basis; that is, the challenge is presented by the federal government, for example, and is only available when local and regional commitments are made. Of course, some funding is available from the state and municipal governmental levels in and of themselves and not necessarily dependent upon resources at another level of government.

It is important to realize that funding should not be dependent upon a single source. Funding patterns and priorities change. Many agencies dependent upon a single source for funding are out of business almost overnight when grants are depleted and not renewed; staff persons drift from one agency to another seeking new challenges and opportunities. Organizations and agencies can best weather the storms of change when their funding is programmed from all five sectors of the philanthropic process, namely, individuals, foundations, corporations, organizations, and government.

Funding mission in the twentieth century is a science unto itself, and few are prepared to engage in the process of financial development. By and large, the church and its related agencies are administered by theologians and program people. Development is not a part of their discipline. Yet along the professional way, they simply cannot conduct their mission for the want of resources. Like it or not, their mission will depend upon their personal involvement in the development process. But leadership in this area must come from the administrator or administration. And those responsible as administrators or leaders in the administration process simply must gain expertise in funding mission or contract for expertise in the area that will enable the organization to undergird ministry and mission with adequate resources.

6

Budgeting Resources

Budgeting processes for organized religion in the United States are deplorable. Hardly an organization on earth is as poorly managed in the budgetary processes as the local church.

THE EXISTING MODEL

Three elements are almost universally present and govern decisions in the budget-making process:

1. The budget of the preceding year is used as the matrix for the new budget. Item by item, line by line, there is a consistency in the budget that has been carried out not only year by year but from generation to generation.

There is little opportunity for organizational growth and change when an organization's life is governed almost entirely by the past. View the budget of your church this year. Compare it with the budgets in each decade of your congregation's life. Line by line, and item by item, there is a continuity in the identification of elements within them. Little imagination. Little growth. Little incentive for greater outreach in striving toward the Kingdom of God. As one views such an annual budget, the words of the writer of Ecclesiastes come almost unbidden to mind: "There is nothing new under the sun."

The past may be prologue to the future, but when it becomes the determining factor for ministry and mission, we are programming obsolescence in a period of history when religion cannot afford such a luxury. To keep abreast of the times, the church simply must be alert to the changing moment, and the budget must not only accommodate change in ministry and mission but anticipate the changes that will inevitably occur in the course of an ensuing year.

2. The budget is limited so that only a modest asking needs to be made of the constituency. *Austerity* is the word most often used in such budgets. Local church leadership seems to believe that the only reasonable asking is modest asking and that Christian stewardship requires the cheapest in everything from salaries to toilet paper. Nothing is too expensive for kings and governors, but nothing is too cheap for God and our Blessed Savior!

Through the years organized religion has exercised a role of advocacy in fair employment practices, working conditions, and salaries for employees in the secular world. It has preached, it has documented, and it has made bold announcements. They have been seen and heard in industry, agriculture, commerce, and government. But the churches are mute on the needs of employees within their organization. The concept of the "suffering servant" has been carried from Calvary to the local church, and everyone on the church's payroll is expected to work more out of love for the Savior than out of love for their families and the provision of adequate resources to accommodate a reasonable and proper life-style in society today.

Church leadership generally is of the opinion that a primary function is to protect the purses of folk in their constituency. Most are capable of protecting their own purses and are fully prepared to engage in the decision-making process as to what they will fund and what they will not fund. Generally they will fund much more than leadership assumes, and church leadership is guilty of not providing the most adequate resources for mission as a result of their protectiveness of their people.

3. The projected income figure will not match anticipated expenditures that appear to be minimal in terms of the organization's need.

When the budget figures are assimilated, based on the past year, and an honest effort to protect the purses of the people in the parish has been made, the minimum need normally exceeds the commitments and the estimated resources that will be available, especially as one considers the parish needs that were not included in the budget matrix from last year. Among these may have been such major items as major repair, updating equipment, or a salary increase that went along with a change in pastoral leadership. (It is on such occasions that salaries tend to take their greatest leap toward adequate compensation for professional staff.)

In the course of the campaign for resources, which most often is by mail and sometimes by personal visitations, there are those who are not contacted as well as those who do not respond. There are many reasons for this, and a great number of them are legitimate: illness, absence from the community, competing demands for people's time, and, at times, inclement weather. As a result there is a shortfall in commitments to meet the minimal askings in terms of the budget for the next fiscal year. Although cuts will be made, it does not appear to be practical to exercise that discipline at the very beginning. Therefore, those responsible for the budget inflate the income projections to accommodate the liabilities that may be incurred. Estimates are made optimistically of income from those who do not pledge, the loose offerings, and income from other sources such as new members, visitors, and perhaps a bequest or two in the course of the year. And when there is not a bequest, it is most likely that the budget will be underexpended in the course of the year not because the budget items have been more than

adequate or the need less than anticipated, but simply because limited resources in cash flow would not permit the
expenditure, however deserving and important it may be.

As a result of these three processes, we discover congregation after congregation suffering from poor facilities, inadequate equipment, and less than adequate leadership in
both ability and number simply because the budget process
is not right. We need to make an about-face in this, and we
need to do it now. The place to begin is in the budget
process.

A PATTERN FOR THE FUTURE

In the world of business, the budget-building process
consists of a five-column model. The first column includes
the budget for the particular item for the preceding year.
The second column includes the amount expended against
that budget item in the preceding year. The third column
lists the amount for the budget item in the current year.
The fourth column provides information of expenditure
against that item in the current year to date (usually the
end of the month preceding the budget-making process).
The fifth column is open to accommodate a figure for the
next year.

A projected income schedule is appended to the budget
working paper wherein projected funding is identified for
each budget item. The projection may consist of budgeted
funds, grants, special gifts, or resources to be developed
from yet-to-be-determined sources. In each event the particular projection is defined as firm, probable, possible, or
soft.

Each budgeted item, as well as resource projection,
emerges from the divisional and departmental personnel responsible for administration. And in each event the "buck
stops" with the individual responsible for the particular
budgeted item.

We would do well to consider such elements in the

budget-building process that will expedite the development of resources and provide credibility for ministry and mission today.

1. Input for the budget-building processes must come from the program units of the organization. Usually the budgeting process begins with the staff, then the facilities are considered, and whatever may be gained beyond that is considered for program. The program element must come first! We can justify neither staff nor facilities unless both are subordinate to the program. The program is of supreme importance!

Feeding into the budget-building process should be the departmental budgets for every program area in the organization that depends in any way upon the core budget of the institution. Actually, it includes every single organization that shares in the use of the facilities, equipment, and staff. Let us list a few that would likely be identified in every local congregation:

The Church (Sunday) School
   Departments
   Classes
The Vacation Church (Bible) School
The Youth Groups
The Choir
The Worship Committee
The Women's Association
   Circles
   Clubs
The Men's Organizations
   Chapters
   Clubs
The Committees of the Boards
The Scouting and Community-related Organizations
All others

We will all agree that certain of these can logically share

in the budget-building process by virtue of the fact that the program and funding for which they are responsible is integrally related to the church and its program. However, every organization that lays claim to the church's time, equipment, and staff must identify the demands that it must make on the local church (its sponsoring, or parent organization) to sustain its purpose. While we do not usually consider these claims as a part of the central budget of the church, they are significant and certainly represent a cost obligation, however remote, that simply must be funded by the local church.

Here there should be some cost accounting. In this a number of factors are important.

What space requirements will there be in the course of the year? What will it cost?

What facilities and equipment will be required in the course of the year? What will they cost?

What staff person's involvement will be required in the course of the year? Clergy? Secretary? Custodian? For example, in the case of the Cub Scouts, the clergy will probably be required to share in the ceremonial. That will represent a half day, or two evenings, per year. A requisition needs to be placed in the organization for this amount of the pastor's time. This will have to be priced and a determination made as to the cost of such service, whether the cost is picked up by the organization or is met by the core budget itself. Organizational functions make demands on staff time continuously, and we simply must recognize the fact that these need to be requisitioned and priced. In time, then, a determination will be made concerning priorities and the askings that can be met and the askings that simply will not be met because of the limitations that make it impossible to meet them.

What supplies will be required in the course of a year? What will they cost?

What new needs exist that would help the program become more effective and more meaningful to the constituency? Which needs should be reduced or eliminated? Which need to be strengthened? All these are of tremendous importance in the budget-building process.

2. Input of research, evaluation, and planning groups must be sought and utilized. Research is basic to the effectiveness of organizations, and studies and surveys must be undertaken in the area of the local church's work and the community or communities it is to serve.

Research findings, of course, will be fed into the organizational structure presently existing. But there is much that simply cannot be limited to existing structures. Certain needs will of necessity be met by several units in the organizational structure. And often the organizational structure simply cannot meet existing needs with the present organizational structure.

Organizational needs must be defined and met if the organization is to be effective in its mission. At times it will require the expanding of program and services in a particular organization. At times it will require the dividing of an organizational structure to accommodate the purpose. At other times a new instrumentality simply must be created if the organization's life is to be effective.

Research and organization simply cannot take place without planning. Planning is an integral part of the process, and usually organizations do little or no planning in terms of organization, structure, and purpose. Practically all the planning that takes place in a local church is focused upon particular events—and even those are not considered from the standpoint of need or outreach. Rather, program for program's sake. We are likely to be impressed with the fact that the posture of the church and church-related organizations remains unchanged.

Continually there is a need to survey both parish and community need. Just as the age of each person changes annually and one out of every five families moves in a single year, changes in the community and organizational life are inevitable.

Even though property values change, residences in a community do not necessarily escalate with each increase in property value and each change of occupant. We need to be mindful of the fact that by and large our property values actually are not increasing. It is the value of our money that is decreasing. Although homes in a parish community sell for a larger sum to each successive occupant, the vocational stature of each new resident does not always equal that of the previous family. A church has been organized and structured to minister to a particular life-style group. As the groupings and life-styles change, the organization must recognize and accommodate those changes or it will be out of touch with people and out of focus in mission. Actually this is what happened to the so-called mainline churches, which simply are not mainline churches anymore. They are no longer mainline in number or mainline in economic worth, and they are certainly not mainline in projecting an effective, vital witness.

The budgetary processes defined from the programmatic aspect and the results of qualified research, evaluation, and planning will bring renewal and hope to the established organizations and opportunities for mission beyond the fondest dream.

Now that we have considered the budget-building process from this base, we can consider those other matters that are important to developing a meaningful budget to ensure capable mission and outreach.

BUILDINGS AND FACILITIES, AND STAFF

Two basics that usually occupy a place of primary consideration in our traditional budgetary processes now emerge after these other considerations: buildings, facilities, and equipment; and staff or personnel. Let us consider them one at a time.

Buildings, facilities, and equipment. In considering the

program units and their definition of needs, we mentioned space, facilities, and equipment. These, however, were confined to a particular departmental need. Now we face the problem of determining the budgetary needs in terms of the institution itself. The building. The furnishings. The instruments, equipment, and supplies.

Consider the existing plant. How old is it? The ordinary life expectancy of buildings in our Western civilization for computation purposes is fifty years. Schedules must be established for painting and decorating, replacing carpets and floor coverings, tuck-pointing the masonry, and other important maintenance needs. If rooms must be painted every six years, one sixth of the cost should be incorporated into each year's budget. If the carpet is to be replaced every twelve years, one twelfth of the cost should be incorporated into each year's budget. If the church is to be tuck-pointed every twenty-five years, or a new roof installed, one twenty-fifth of these costs should be incorporated into each year's budget. No church is fiscally sound, or exercising good stewardship of its resources and property, if it is not budgeting in each year the fair share of operating and maintaining the property.

Proper maintenance will certainly enhance the property and facilities and, even more important, extend the years over which they may be used. Indeed, the useful life of a building may be extended to one, two, or three hundred years.

Now if a local congregation will adequately fund maintenance and improvement, the insuring needs may not seem as great. However, the insurability of the property will increase and there will be greater opportunity to expand both facilities and program in the event of a loss.

An important fact emerges in our consideration of the funding strategy and need. All churches are not new. In fact, practically all of them have been used for many years, and some, in fact, have actually served beyond the years of normal usage.

Here we need to begin where we are in terms of the organizational plant life. If the replacement of a structure is budgeted on fifty-year replacement, and the building is twenty-five years old now, the budgeted amount for replacement should be elevated to 200 percent.

Periodically the annual increment must be increased to accommodate inflation. If every fourth year the sum is increased by 25 percent, this will compensate for the inflationary factor of 6.25 percent per year (noncompounded). A figure between those of the inflationary indexes in 1977 and 1978 would certainly suffice.

There will be much resistance to this type of budgeting in many local churches, for there is the assumption that those who have the vision to build facilities should pay for the facilities. I would perhaps concur with this attitude if in the intervening years people were to assume like obligations to expand ministry and mission. They simply do not. In the intervening years the church is engaged largely in a housekeeping process, and this is entirely inconsistent with Christian commitment. From this standpoint Christianity is truly a sleeping giant.

The formula for the replacement of buildings, then, is the replacement of the building on a fifty-year actuarial with the annual rate accruing to provide full funding for replacement at the fifty-year milestone and added increments compounded at 25 percent every four years. This will provide evidence of fiscal integrity in organizational life.

Staff and personnel. Staff and personnel is another most important matter for consideration in the budgeting of resources. Organizations generally do not give consideration to what they need. Rather, they fall into the trap of identifying positions considered normal for a religious organization and proceed to build a program on those capabilities rather than to build staff on community, organizational, and/or institutional needs. So when we think of a local church, we think of pastors, a secretary, an organist/music director, and a sexton. Why? Because every religious organization has them.

Has it ever occurred to you that many churches would be better off without a pastor? A first response to the question is, "What of pastoral care?" Just how much pastoral care do the clergy provide in our society today? "Little, or none, for most of the church members" is the answer that any scientific survey would disclose. There may be much for a very few. Some for a limited number. None for most.

I believe that this illustrates the fact that we should structure staff needs from the standpoint of the parishioners. But what of pastoral care? Pastoral care is actually the caring of a concerned community, and the concerned community is the membership, not the employed persons relating to a membership constituency, in the local church.

The caring community is personified by the pastor, but the real caring is done not by the clergy but by those whose lives interweave from pew to pew and meeting to meeting. The church that is truly great, and the church that provides real pastoral ministry, is the church where members relate to one another, where hearts are warmed through fellowship, and where burdens are lifted by expressions of care and concern.

As the needs for facilities and equipment arise out of the program, so the needs for personnel in terms of clergy and staff members emerge from the program that is to be developed and maintained to accomplish the church's mission.

Generally we are using a few folk with limited skills to lead the church's mission. Their responsibilities are so broad and so diverse that most are unable to exercise their skills in the area of excellence and are required to use their talents in areas where they are limited in ability and have little or no interest. This is the result of the insistence of the churches that each one have full-time employees to carry on the full mission of the church.

Every organization could be better served and led if it contracted for expert leadership in limited areas on a contractual basis for a limited time. In some cases this would be by the week; in others, by the month, by the quarter, or on a semiannual or annual basis.

In limited ways we have done this with financial secretaries, organists-directors, secretaries, and sometimes clergy. But here the concept has been restricted because the emphasis has been on economy and not on excellence, on availability and not on capability.

Few churches have sought the very best expertise for the task. Rather, they have asked who is available to do a minimal task for the least amount of money. As a result, most of their positions are extremely overpaid—not that the remuneration is too great for the time they spend but that it is too great for the responsibility they are to assume based on their ability and experience. Many are prisoners of time. They merely do a job because they are expected to fill a time frame rather than accomplish a purpose.

What capabilities do we need in a parish? Many. It would be impossible to list them all. We can list a few.

We need preaching ministers. Preachers who can communicate the Gospel, compete with the communicators in the mass media, and feed souls.

We need counselors. Professional people who can deal with human-spiritual problems and who are qualified to guide those who are personally troubled or distressed.

We need visitors. Trained persons who excel in the art of conversation and who project a warmth of concern and receptiveness to the needs of people.

We need social workers to guide persons through the maze of political and social structures to meet the needs that will enable them to attain the objective toward which they are reaching as well as an honorable life.

We need public relations experts capable of projecting the church's mission and purpose beyond the stained glass windows and cold gray stone of the ecclesiastical heritage.

We need teachers capable of teaching the Gospel and enabling individuals to grow in "wisdom, and in stature, and in favor with God and man."

We need musicians skilled in the music of the church and expert in the liturgical instrumentalities of these times.

We need maintenance and equipment experts who are trained to care for facilities and oversee the stewardship of resources available to those sharing in the opportunities presented by the parish.

We need administrators to oversee the business and financial operations of the organization. While good business leaders are elected to the boards of the church, they seem to lose all good business sense when they enter the church. The fact that the church survives at all with so little business expertise is one of the miracles of the age. Good administration is important to the fiscal integrity and credibility of the organization.

Through the years some churches have played at the game of sharing leadership. It has seldom been tested simply because it has grown out of the need of limited resources rather than from the desire to excel in more excellent ways. The objective has been wrong inasmuch as the direction has usually been to accommodate the past with accepted patterns and structures rather than to fulfill mission, purpose, effectiveness, and service. Seldom do we approach programming from the standpoint of need and service. Rather, we approach it from the standpoint of what others are doing or from the standpoint of the past, little realizing that all others are doing the same thing. The matrix emerges from the past with little or no effectiveness, and the church moves more and more into obsolescence and irrelevance.

The epitaph of the future is "failure" if the church continues in its present direction. We can no longer accept the luxury of programs accommodating resources and reducing services month by month, year by year, to match the funds available from folk who give out of convenience from modest cash flow. If it were not for the dedication of a few, as limited as it sometimes tends to be, the church would have been out of business a long time ago. Often the product is poor, the performance is weak, the program irrelevant. The budgeting of resources to match needs, and the development of resources to support mission appropriate to the life and times of which we are a part, will move the church from strength to strength as it approaches the finest hour to be complementary to the God of all creation and the Christ who died to save us all.

7

Exercising
Stewardship

Stewardship is no new term in the church. Perhaps of all the terms used in the church, it is one most frequently identified and understood by the membership at large. It is a term that deals with church support, finance, resources, and time and is a term that is used almost exclusively for commitment among members and not for the institution itself. In this respect organized religion does a better job of conveying its message than it does of exercising an adequate discipline over its property, facilities, equipment, resources, and time.

Let us move the term from others to self, from the communicant to the organization, from the people to the institution.

THE STEWARDSHIP OF PROPERTY

What image comes into focus for you as you consider the term *church?* It may be a great cathedral with impressive towers or churches built of stone with leaded glass windows. It may be a white building with a towering steeple and plain glass windows to let in the light and permit the

worshiper to view the world of nature. For most it will
tend to be an image of their particular church or of an impressive structure that they may have visited in one of the
great cities of the world. But think of the term *churches*.
Here the image changes and becomes less clear, and as we
tend to concentrate, less desirable patterns emerge on our
consciousness suggestive of obsolescence, neglect, and need
for repair.

Visit almost any church and tour the plant. You are
apt to find stained walls, chipped plaster, and areas much in
need of decorating. There will be evidence in places that
the roof leaks, the windows are in need of repair, and the
floors are in need of resurfacing or recovering. In all likelihood there has been a major improvement program in the
past ten years and there will be another one in the next
decade. Certain needed repairs and improvements were
not made last time, and certain ones will not be completed
next time. Continuously the church is dependent upon the
past and the future. The present plant has been funded by
folk in the past, and major repairs are anticipated to be
made by folk in the future. It is an unheard-of thing for
each generation in Christendom to assume only its fair
share and for each annual budget to reflect the sums required to exercise good stewardship in each and every year.

Church administrators would be wise to establish a
formula providing for the repair and replacement of the
church. Here are some suggestions, based on a broad survey
of church plant replacement needs and costs.

ITEM	PERCENT PER ANNUM
Repair and replacement of physical structure	2
Repair and replacement of stained glass windows	3
Repair and replacement of sanctuary furniture	2

Repair and replacement of sanctuary carpet	7½
Repair and replacement of kitchen equipment and utensils	6
Repair and replacement of sidewalks and parking areas	4

Presently congregations find it necessary to have a capital-funds drive every fifteen to twenty years to meet the basic responsibilities of the parish for repairs and improvements. Most fund drives are inadequate, since we expect a congregation to do in three years what it should have been doing over a period of ten to fifteen years. And because of decay and neglect, the work is more costly than it should have been.

Most local church equipment and church structures are insured, but most often inadequately. The insurance policies, however, provide no funding for the ordinary replacement needs of a congregation. They provide protection in case of fire, flood, or natural disasters. But most facilities are not visited by wind, water, or flame. Their story is "insured but not preserved." It ought to be "insured and preserved," regardless of what the cause might be.

Suppose we take the repair and replacement schedule suggested above and provide askings, or guidelines, for personal estate planning to pick up the slack for forsaken and forgotten years. A church building cost $100,000 to build and it is thirty years old. A $60,000 bequest will do much to provide an endowment for the facility if an additional $2000 per year is placed in the budget for this purpose. Stained glass windows in a church ten years old cost $10,000 to install. A bequest of $3000 will bring the endowment fund to a current level, and $300 per year added to the endowment fund for the annual budget will insure their future.

A complete inventory should be made of the church and its facilities to determine the amount that would be required to provide capital resources large enough to compensate for the building at the present time.

Local church officers would do well to study the annual reports of major corporations for guidelines in this respect. In 1977, as an example, 4 percent of the gross earnings of Polaroid, 5 percent of the gross earnings of Dan River Mills, and 6 percent of the gross earnings of Borden went toward the depreciation and replacement of property, facilities, and equipment.

We recommended in the previous chapter that each annual budget incorporate such funding as will be required to ensure the plant's being cared for in a manner consistent with its original appearance.

In the event that the church has not taken steps to provide for replacement, repair, or improvement, a goal for bequested income would be that sum of money that would have been accumulated to this moment in time if proper fiscal practices had been exercised over the life and work of the church since the present building was built.

In practical terms this means that we simply must look to bequested income, as well as to capital gifts, to accomplish the task. Across the church I meet many people who do not believe in an endowment fund. They believe that the church's needs should be met by the local congregation and that the officers should spend all that the members provide. This seems strange to me, for they are not reluctant to receive from the past the building, the altar, the pews, and the musical instruments. Yet, if a tragedy were to occur, they would need to dip into their own pockets to replace any or all of them. Why is it that we expect families to be self-sufficient but assume that in the event of a crisis it is proper for a church to dip into the savings of the members rather than into the savings of the institution—which it must have if it is to have any fiscal integrity at all?

In institutes, seminars, and workshops I have insisted that a church should have in reserves, as liquid assets, an amount equal to 200 percent of the annual budget. Beyond that, it can invest those capital gifts in mission beyond the

four walls. This does not mean that I believe that a parish
has no responsibility for mission beyond its four walls until
it attains that sum. Indeed, it is not likely that it can ever
attain that sum unless it is mature enough to have identified
its mission across the nation and around the world throughout its entire program and history. But this is the magnitude
of the sum that providence requires.

This figure of 200 percent of the annual budget is in addition to those capital reserves that will be required to replace the plant, the facilities, and the equipment at least in
the proportions to which each has been used in assessing
projections of service capability. If the replacement costs
for a church would today equal $1 million against perhaps a
$2-million ultimate replacement value, and if the annual
budget is $150,000, that church would be on target in
terms of my projection when the endowment has reached
a figure of $1.3 million.

One says, "That is a lot of money for a church to have."
Actually, the church has a great asset already. However,
because of depreciation and disrepair, the physical asset is
not as great as it has been in years past or as great as it
should be at the present time.

It is difficult to avoid the feeling that adequate stewardship of resources has an important role in the impact the
church can expect to have in its community and on the
larger society in which it lives.

THE STEWARDSHIP OF FACILITIES

When we talk about property, we tend to think of real
estate. When we talk about equipment, we tend to think of
furnishings. But between real estate and equipment there
are the facilities that facilitate the life and mission of the
church.

Parking facilities. These have become increasingly important to local churches as public transportation has been

scaled down considerably at the very times that it is most needed by folk sharing in the worship and program of the local church. Private transportation is practically inseparable from church participation. There is no way that most persons can share in the church's program if they cannot drive or ride with someone else, and they must have a place to park when they get there.

In most cases the need for parking facilities throughout the seven days of each week has been spotty. In the vast majority of cases, the peak need exists only perhaps six to ten hours in each week. For the greater part of the week, the church parking lot is a considerably underutilized facility. With limited resources, local churches have looked to the parking lot as an area of financial development helpful to the world of commerce and important to the fiscal integrity of the organization. Here the church needs to exercise great care lest it become entangled in the difficult issue of the separation of church and state. Basically the church wants both tax exemption for its parking lot and the income those parking areas can provide when the capacity exceeds their need. Some municipalities have provided an abatement in taxes for the parking area calculated on the percentage of the lot and time proportioned to the religious and sacramental mission of the church. Some churches, in lieu of taxes, have made a contribution to the municipal government for the services provided to the tax-exempt organizations.

Whether the church should provide such a convenience at all to the members of the church and other folk participating in their programs depends upon the organization's ability to maintain the area in a reasonable and proper manner. If the maintenance of such a facility is a drag on the organization and a drain on the organization's resources, it should not.

Here the religious organizations need to reconsider the purpose and establish priorities to ensure that they are on target in effectively supporting the mandate under which they must operate as the body of Christ. How crucial to the success of vital program is the existence of the parking facility?

The church needs to exercise good stewardship over the parking areas for which it has responsibility and to take care of those facilities. They need to be weighed fairly in terms of the church's life and mission and in terms of the portion of the asset that may reasonably be assigned to that facility in terms of the capital outlay, the operating budget of the organization, and the social purposes for which the church has been established.

Recreational facilities. Recreational facilities are another component in the church's life and mission. Often recreation is considered simply in secular terms. However, recreation is very much a spiritual process and inseparable from the commandment given to the first persons to renew and replenish the earth. The Christian Mission is not only a mission to redeem fallen man but to engage in the redemptive process that will redeem the whole person spiritually, morally, physically, mentally, and socially.

The facilities for recreation may include gymnasiums, swimming pools, and bowling alleys. They may include parlors, game rooms, and activity centers. They may also include equipment such as checkerboards, decks of cards, or a record player. If properly used, they are all legitimate parts of the church's facilities. Worship and education must permeate the recreational and renewal processes, and the recreation and renewal must permeate the whole worship and education process. This requires careful budgeting, adequate planning, and sound supervision. Nothing contributes more to a negative image of the church among many of our young people than recreational equipment that has been abused and inadequately maintained—a shuffleboard with broken pucks, a deck of cards from which one card is missing, or a cue stick too badly warped to be of any use.

All too often these are signs that we have been playing

at God's work and are not taking seriously the mission of the church in all its aspects.

Recreation, and re-creation, if considered important to ministry and mission, must be taken seriously, be in good order, and complementary to the Gospel.

THE STEWARDSHIP OF EQUIPMENT

As important as buildings and facilities are, they are of little value without equipment.

Literary, research, and resource materials constitute an area in which the stewardship of equipment is often inadequate. Much is published in the field of religion, and some of the greatest scholarly work in history has been produced by theologians in such areas as biblical, moral, and ethical research. But all too often one would not be aware of this from visiting a library in a local church. The books generally are those left by former pastors or provided to the church as personal property of little or no value from the estates of deceased members. The books are not cataloged or arranged in a fashion consistent with that of the public library or libraries in educational institutions.

This is a tragedy, for organized religion has been a parent in the learning processes. Education in our society began in the church and matured in the religious institutions. Administration in the local church must give serious consideration to the development of adequate resource material for its constituency. A good place to begin would be to incorporate a library with current standard references. A survey of services would further indicate the particular types of reference materials that would be essential as resources for the leadership and participants. As these are identified, and the need for them made known, special gifts as well as memorials will complement budget allocations that may be modest to begin with.

Library materials should be properly arranged, cataloged, and programmed for short-term borrowing when necessary.

A library need not be large to be effective. Quality is more important than quantity.

Too frequently audiovisual resources are in the same condition as the materials in our church libraries. In many cases the equipment is old, inadequate, and in disrepair. There is little in the budget for film rentals, and usually the films shown are those available without cost from a denomination, ecumenical organization, or library. Sound administration demands significant funding to permit the development of model programs with efficient equipment and significant programming. Only in this way can audiovisual programming play its rightful role in education and communication.

Musical instruments also are among equipment over which sound stewardship needs to be exercised. Pipe organs, electronic instruments, and pianos are the instruments of the modern church, but they require adequate maintenance and care if they are to play their role in the life of the congregation.

Even the smallest pipe organ is a complex and delicate instrument. It is highly sensitive to changes in temperature and humidity. If it is to be satisfactory at all, it must be installed with care and maintained on a regular schedule.

Electronic instruments generally do not require the maintenance of the pipe organs they have been designed to replace. Some may require special instruction if their full potential is to be realized, since their stops are not always identical with those commonly used on the pipe organ, but usually a person can move from a pipe organ to an electronic instrument with little difficulty. Manufacturers consider that feature an important one as music committees select an instrument for local churches. Beyond this, the change of a tube or the replacement of a speaker may be all that is required. But they must be cared for adequately.

Pianos present a special challenge to the local church. They are frequently gifts of families who no longer have use for them, and they are often in poor repair at the time they are contributed. Once in the church, they may be subjected to wide variations in temperature and humidity and to abuse by untrained players. Those charged with the acceptance of such gifts should make certain that the pianos are in good condition or of such a quality that they can be brought up to standard with resources available either through the regular budget or by some special commitment.

Contracts for servicing the instruments should be established to provide reasonable and proper care. Here local organizations would do well to consider contractual arrangements for services with other organizations and agencies in the same area in order that quality service may be sustained at the most economical cost. While each contract may well be independent of the others, such pooling arrangements can reduce travel time and make for greater efficiency as well as economy in providing service to particular organizations.

Equipment in the sanctuary? Consider the pews. How often have women walked out of a church annoyed because the rough places have snagged another pair of hose? The pew cushions themselves are not clean and the hymnals and/or Bibles worn and torn. Appointments in the chancel are often unkept. Paraments are faded and sometimes ragged. Conditions in the choir loft are usually not any better. Here, too, the music is worn and torn—more abused than used. Robes are cleaned less often than they should be; some are older than others and frequently of a different shade, resulting from differing dates of acquisition as well as frequency of use.

Equipment in the parlors is often in no better condition. It generally consists of residential furnishings subject to what we may well define as "commercial" use, and it simply cannot endure the use and abuse the public gives it. In many cases it is living on borrowed time.

In defense of the church, the plant, the facilities, and the equipment, we must simply be mindful of the fact that public property does not belong to anyone. Public property belongs to everyone. The result is that public property is terribly abused and misused wherever the public has access to it. Government buildings, public schools, community centers, and churches are all in the same sphere. Most people are considerate of them once in a while, but for the most part it is all subject to abuse much of the time.

Administrators and administration must recognize, too, the fact that many persons elected to responsible positions in organized religion are not educated or trained to assume the responsibility given to them. Few elected as elders, deacons, vestrypersons, and/or trustees have experience in or outside the church. Dedicated and capable in their particular area of expertise, they assume responsibilities in organized religion for which they are not prepared. As an example, a hospital employs a superintendent or administrator. This person is educated and qualified for the position. Equipment and supplies are requisitioned and ordered in terms of established practices in which the person has been schooled. Institutional furniture and furnishings are ordered according to standards that meet specifications in which the superintendent or administrator has been schooled.

It is not unusual for a church board to meet and order supplies and equipment in which the assessment is made entirely on the basis of personal domestic experience and tastes. Many of the supplies and equipment ordered by the churches, and often by related agencies, would not meet the minimum standards for institutional use. While they are often costly to begin with, they become even more costly in the long run, inasmuch as replacement is required much sooner than had proper commercial/institutional equipment been secured in the first place.

This is not the shame of those assuming positions of leadership and responsibility in the local church and related agencies. In most cases they are innocent. It does alert us to the fact, however, that those who assume responsibility in the church and church-related agencies need to be educated and trained and that part of the administrative responsibility is to train and educate persons to responsible decisions.

This does not mean that as persons are installed in positions of leadership or elected to membership on boards a training school must be organized or classes scheduled for special instruction. It does mean that the administrator must be mindful of the fact that each meeting will likely require special education through the ordinary processes of committee functions and that supporting material must be available to be shared with individuals in assisting them to a full understanding of quantity, quality, and excellence in materials, equipment, and supplies that will prove their worth in the service of the Master.

The educational processes in board and committee meetings, valid decisions as corporate directors, more adequate reserves through bequested income, and sound annual budget processes are key instrumentalities to exercising wise stewardship in organizational life and work. The administrator (and administration) is the key to valid and successful processes.

8

Facilitating
Objectives

One cannot facilitate objectives without first identifying what those objectives are. In the course of the first seven chapters, we have been opening the doors to an understanding of what some objectives might be and the importance of such objectives to the life and work of the church and/or organization. They are, of course, equally important to the mission of the church and individuals in the household of faith. But we have been dealing with objectives in general and not necessarily with objectives in particular. It is as a sermon addressed against sin. It becomes an effective instrument only as it focuses on particular sins.

The church needs to claim its identity. It needs to establish both short-term and long-term goals. It needs to comprehend the potential, as well as the means, of funding mission on the local, national, and world levels. And it needs to exercise good stewardship not only in the development of resources but in the management of those things—fiscal and physical—committed to its care.

IDENTIFYING OBJECTIVES

Let us begin by identifying objectives.
Here, in organization, we suffer a great hardship. Or-

ganizational objectives tend to become personal objectives, and personal objectives tend to become organizational objectives. This may best be illustrated in terms of pastoral leadership. Pastoral leadership tends to be little more than the imposing of a pastor's will, program, and priorities upon an organization's life and work. Real leadership demands expertise in the process of directing a group to a common understanding and the identification of common goals and objectives as well as determining the means by which they may be attained.

Many times folk in local churches speak concerning the program of the church under previous pastors. Usually the leader is seen as responsible. It was his (or her) idea. We could not have done it without him (or her). The converse is also true. We did it. We concurred with those ideas. He (or she) could not have done it without us. The tragedy of the two is that often the group process is not permitted to work and the results are far less successful, or effective, than they could be if the process becomes, indeed, the heart and the mind of the group.

In a parish of a thousand members, certainly all will not, or cannot, be involved with the process. But lay leadership must be involved in the process. Input that represents the community at large as well as the parish itself must be available. There must be input from those who may be outside the formal membership but who are a part of the larger constituency of the congregation. While a church is a gathered society, it is never an island entire unto itself.

While we cannot here define who shall participate in the process of identifying objectives, we can at least insist that the persons not be limited to the organizational leaders, the official board, the board of directors, or even just the congregation. There must be a cross-fertilization of ideas, concerns, and needs, and in this event one could well begin by establishing a cabinet of concerns. Here there would be representation from the clergy and staff, the official boards, the organizations, the parish, and the parish community. One will soon discover that as folk from the "outside" are included in the process they become an intrinsic part of the organization.

Once a cabinet, or decision-making group, is structured, it is important that it define a course for the future, both in short-term and long-term objectives. To a degree, the long-term objectives may well be the first step, inasmuch as short-term goals will be required as a series of steps to reach each of the long-term objectives. Here planning is weakened when the goals are ill defined, i.e., when the goals are defined in such general terms that it is impossible for an individual or a group to relate to them. In defining the goals, one should seek objectives that are reasonable, feasible, and challenging. Apply three questions:

1. Is it in the realm of the possible? If it is not, the process will fail. Here we will need to consider the person-power that will be required to attain the objective. Financial resources will in all likelihood be a consideration. The time frame, too, is important. If goal attainment is too far removed from the point of personal involvement, benefit, and/or appreciation, it is too removed from personal experience to gain the participation that it will require to meet the objective.

2. Is it feasible? There must be a feasibility study. Most often in the business world such studies are conducted by experts on a contractual basis. Costs are recovered through rate structures. However, in the church such experts are not readily available and most churches have not determined the means of recovering the cost for the same. But a feasibility study must be made—perhaps not a formal one, but at least a serious consideration of the criteria to determine the practicality of the idea and/or objective. Here one will require a complete inventory ranging from people to capability, finance to resources, facilities to equipment. While feasibility may tend to eliminate some goals and objectives, it is more likely to modify them to accommodate the realities in the situation.

3. Is it challenging? If there is no challenge, there will be

no response. The objective must be worthwhile. It must make a difference. It must generate enthusiasm. It must cause persons and groups to reach beyond their present state or situation. Once attained, it must provide a deep sense of satisfaction that the end did indeed justify the means.

The cabinet, or planning group, having determined the short- and long-term objectives and having faced the three questions and obtained reasonable answers, must proceed to the implementation process. Remember, the cabinet is not the board of directors. It is the think tank.

SELLING THE IDEA

Having considered the possibility and feasibility of the plan and the challenge it provides, the cabinet must then determine the empowering or enabling process. What body has the power to incorporate the goal into the organization's program design for the future? In the corporate sector it might be a branch, subsidiary, or department, and the particular governing body responsible for the same. In some churches and organizations the process is rather simple. A single board is responsible for the total decision-making process. However, one must be certain that this is indeed a fact. Seldom does a single board have such power and influence in and of itself. Even though there may not be other formally constituted boards, it is likely that there are organizations, groups, and factions that are indeed power blocs in and of themselves. And just because a board reaches a decision to incorporate a new process in the program does not mean that it really happens. It does not really happen until the people who must provide the energy and support are fully on board.

As the cabinet identifies the policy-making group (or groups), there is a need to determine the approach that is to be taken to sell the group on the idea. This selection process is most important. In most cases there is no staff person who can be assigned the responsibility. Selection will involve volunteers. Many times a good idea will simply die because of the person who shares it. This may have nothing to do with whether the person is capable of presenting the idea well. Many ideas have been presented poorly but have gained support readily because the persons presenting the ideas have been the right ones for presenting those particular ideas. Likewise, many ideas have been presented most capably—with polish, clear definition, and unquestionable expertise—but have been turned down simply because of the person making the presentation. The causes may not be in the organization itself. A conflict of personalities in a service club on a Monday may destroy a person's effectiveness in a church organization the following Sunday, and for many Sundays thereafter.

In selecting the right person to present the idea, we must focus on both the idea and the person. Is the idea right for this person? Is this person right for this idea? There must be a perfect marriage between the two.

While the selection of the person to present the idea, or plan, is important, it is also important to select the time. Former President Richard M. Nixon stated that he became president of the United States because he happened to be "at the right place at the right time." For some ideas there may never be a right time. But for every idea there are some times that are more favorable than others. And there are some ideas for which only a single time will be right.

Having selected the person (or persons) and the time (or times), it is important to devise the means of presentation. How much of the plan is to be shared at the first meeting? Will it be presented as a total plan or as a first phase in a program? Will it require an immediate decision or is it to be presented for evaluation and feedback?

It is not likely that the decision makers responsible for phasing the idea or plan into the program will be the persons responsible for or capable of carrying out the plan. They may not even be the persons to implement or oversee the plan. Work, then, needs to be done by the cabinet to lay the groundwork among persons capable of implementing at least the first stages of the plan.

Here one needs to be careful that the efforts to implement the process will not seem presumptuous to the decision makers or an act of jumping the gun in getting a job done. Often such considerations may be part of the feasibility study. After all, if no one is interested in the plan or willing to work for the attainment of the objective, there is little reason to present a plan or idea to an empowering body.

Here, too, timing is important. It should not precede the presentation to the board of directors to the degree that work will be delayed. If a plan is shared, work assured, and direction limited, the usual result is disappointment and an unwillingness to resume activity at a later time. Green signals must be evident along the way even though a caution light might be anticipated from time to time. Red lights may not only halt progress for a time but terminate the activity and interest of certain folk for all time.

Consideration needs to be given in these initial stages to funding as well. There is hardly anything that can be done programmatically that does not require financial resources. The financial development process, too, may actually begin before the plan or idea is presented to the governing body in the organization. Some feasibility studies will show that a plan will not be incorporated into the program of an organization unless it is actually funded. In most cases partial funding or verbal commitments supporting the financial feasibility of the project will be adequate.

Many programs will require more facilities and equipment than an organization has. In some cases the plan must include the acquisition of facilities and equipment and in other cases contracting for the use of facilities and equipment belonging to others. In many cases the project will require some of each.

Let us begin with the acquisition of facilities and equipment. Time and price are important considerations here. How soon will the facilities and equipment be needed? Can they be secured in time? Will those available at the time be adequate to do the job? Does the project justify the cost? In many cases the price will never be too high. Programs are important regardless of the price. In all cases the price will seem too high for some, reasonable to others, and almost nominal to others. This will depend upon individual interest and values.

Consider the utilization of facilities and equipment belonging to others. Availability will be one factor. Accountability will be another factor. Suitability will be still another. Also, the duration of the project will be most important. Contracting for facilities and equipment belonging to others may be the most economical course for a process of short duration, but if one is thinking in terms of a period of time extending over many years, the utilization of contracted facilities and equipment may be too costly. When the project or program is to be of short duration, the cost of acquiring facilities and equipment may be entirely out of reason. Planners must consider both courses.

They will also need to consider what effect the character of the organization or institution possessing the equipment and/or facilities may have on the program. Does it enhance the credibility of the offering or does it detract to such a degree that little is accomplished as a result of a contractual arrangement? The image, and projected image, of the sponsoring institution, agency, or organization is very important. For some organizations the identification of the sponsoring agency is crystal clear regardless of where its programs are held. In other cases a program most effectively operated in a facility foreign to the particular agency tends to become identified with the organization with which the program agency contracts rather than with the agency itself. Those projecting the plan must determine how important this factor is in implementing an idea.

TESTING THE CONCEPT

Perhaps the greatest test of an idea is whether or not it consummates a happy marriage with the institution, agency, or organization that is to be responsible for it. Does it really belong? Does it enhance the image? Does it relate to the program? Does it identify well the design of the agency? Certain projects may be of such great significance that they overshadow the agency. The implementation, in a sense, creates a new organization—an image incompatible with the image projected in the past. In corporate life those inappropriate for a particular company are marketed to others. The religious society has never developed a brokerage service to accommodate the transfer of ideas or program potential. In a church they either "go" or "die."

The testing of ideas will play strongly in the evolution of the plan and the decision-making processes that will determine whether or not they may indeed be approved by the governing board in the overall plan and incorporated into the program of the organization.

In the planning processes, as we seek to introduce and develop new programs, it is essential that we facilitate the objectives.

We must identify them.

We must comprehend the possibility, feasibility, and challenge presented through them.

We must determine how they are to be implemented in terms of persons and time.

We must consider their feasibility in terms of persons, finance, facilities, and equipment.

With these accomplishments we should be in a position to expand the program to accommodate the plan and/or project.

9

Expanding Program

The end result of facilitating objectives in existing organizations is usually expanding program. In some cases it may result in the replacement of some program elements. However, even when this occurs, the organization usually finds that the total range of services has enlarged and that the labor load has increased, and the end result in reality is indeed an expanded program.

Most pastors, and executives, believe that it is easier to expand programs than to reduce the program offerings in organizational life. However, in many cases, the situation is not considered objectively, for if it were, it would be clear that program expansion is at least as difficult, and in many cases much more difficult, if leadership, staff, and constituency are to give full consideration and attention to existing programs. Program expansion all too often takes place at the expense of existing programs. This is not intentional, to be sure, but it happens for several reasons:

1. Because a program is new, it is given priority over existing programs and concerns.

2. Staff persons tend to be more enthusiastic about new programs. New staff persons entering into a program espe-

cially sense a challenge as well as an opportunity in the new program offering.

3. Resources tend to be more adequate in terms of expectancy in the newly budgeted activity. While they may not be adequate, they are usually more than adequate at the very beginning, and for the first several months there is little or no pressure to reduce or limit expenditures.

This brings us to the competition that tends to emerge in organizational life as a result of expanded programs. There may be discontent among other staff persons not directly involved in the new program dimension. There may be disappointment in the fact that restricted budgets appear more limited as a result of the new program development, and in many cases they may very well be, as existing budgets are sometimes pared down to accommodate the new or added service. There may be distress in the fact that a new program has been introduced when existing programs frequently are inadequately funded, staffed, and serviced by the organization or agency. The absence of the profit motive, and a resultant advantage to a total corporate well-being, is lost in the voluntary nonprofit agency.

THE MARRIAGE OF THE NEW
AND THE OLD

In order to reduce or limit these competitive elements, important procedures must be followed to ensure harmony and unity among staff persons, and the effectiveness of the organization.

1. The governing body, its leadership and staff, must participate in the development process. There is need for full participation in each stage of organizational development to gain a sense of membership in the process and in the program. Every person must be in a position to claim a portion of the program as a personal idea, a product of his or her thinking as well as work.

2. Individuals must develop a sense of ownership in the organization's operation and in the new program. A person may have participated in the conceptualization and in the very program and purpose without developing a sense of ownership, or proprietorship, in a particular program. This is not enough. Each person must be helped to gain a sense of oneness with the process and an identification with the project as a product of his or her insight as well as initiative.

3. All involved must realize that the new program is not in competition with the overall program. Each segment of programming should be enhanced, and perhaps improved, as a result of the new program offering.

THE IMPORTANCE OF EXPANDING PROGRAMS

Actually, new programming, the expanding of horizons, and the extending of services are indicators of a vibrant, effective, and efficient organization. To stand still is to go backward. To sustain only the services and programs of the past would seem to indicate that the organization is negligent in its duty to serve the present and the future. There is no such thing as standing still. Organizations, like individuals, must grow or die.

New and expanding programs provide opportunity for the organization to project its image, make known its services, and interpret its purposes. When new programs are announced, there is opportunity to restate the services from the past, the origin of the organization, and the operational base from which the new program is to be launched.

An organization should not wait until completely new programs are implemented to make such announcements. It is always proper to redefine mission, reinterpret objectives, and restate purposes. New terms, new personalities, and new emphases are always in order, always newsworthy, and always important to organizational life.

As the program expands within a church or agency, there is, of course, the opportunity for new persons to become involved in the program. However, this should not be the only purpose or the only means of measuring the effectiveness of the program offering. Folk entering a new program will be new to the particular program but may not be new to the organization. They may simply move from one program to another, one function to another, or one group to another. Fortunately, all will not move from the same activity or to the same activity. As a result, even with the same participants in the organizational structure, there will be a new cross-fertilization of ideas, a different exchange of experiences, and sometimes different insights into the very same problems. And growth is certain.

Advertisements in business make new products known and emphasize bargain sales for a few items. Few advertisements are intended only to move sale items. The purpose is to increase sales in every department. New program offerings have this effect in organizational life. A rising tide floats all ships.

Additional folk coming into the organization cannot be assumed to be interested only in the new or expanded program. Rather, the new program offering is the instrumentality that brings them into the total program. As a result of differing experiences, interests, and ideas, some will move from one program to another, from a limited participation in a single aspect of the organization's life to a larger and perhaps full participation in the organization's life and work. This is what I defined in my book *Models for Ministry* to be organizational evangelism. The total organization gains as a result of individuals' becoming involved in a single program, and the single program becomes the means whereby the individual is ushered into a full participation in the organization's life and work. This, indeed, is as it should be.

THE SCOPE FOR EXPANSION

In expanding the program, it is important that the appeal be as broad as the community. Organizations tend to become selective—certainly more selective than business enterprises. They do so to their own harm. They tend to project their image, purpose, and invitation to folk of their own type—folk of their own race, color, creed, national origin, and sometimes sexual preference. This is perhaps the greatest tragedy in organizational structures in the United States today. Each time an individual or a group is excluded, there is a limitation not only to participation by but to the growth of the individuals within the organization itself.

These limitations are especially critical in the local church. A church must minister to its community—not the select community but the geographical community of which it is a part. There is little justification for the tax exemption of religious organizations who conceive of their constituency as other than the persons who occupy their particular geographical area and provide tax payments to cover not only their fair share of the tax burden but also the portion that, on a percentage basis, would be assumed by the church if it were a taxable entity. The people in the community have assumed a responsibility for the church. The church must assume a responsibility for the people in the community! That does not mean some of the people but all of the people! Ministry, mission, and concern must include everyone.

Now it is impossible to expand program without a mindfulness of the dimensions of the community. We have called our society a melting pot. The description is frequently understood to assume a loss of identity to traditions. Such a description is most inadequate. Traditions are sustained —sometimes coerced and sometimes compromised—and the strains of human history are evident in every community; while there may be a denial of their presence, the strains continue without interruption.

Expanding program merely to broaden the defined curricula of the church, organization, or agency is not expanding program in the full sense of the word. Program expansion actually takes place when the program enlarges to reach more completely the perimeters of participant potential and the involvement of the greatest number of persons possible. This is especially evident in the urban scene. When the inner-city churches do this, they thrive and grow. When they do not, they become shadows of their former selves.

Seldom do we find a church that takes seriously an evaluation of need and an expansion in program design to meet those needs. Rather, the local church operates from the matrix of the past, and presumably because it apparently met the needs in ministry and mission in program designs a century or two ago, we assume that it meets the needs in ministry and mission in program design today. Hardly any single field of endeavor finds this true. Why do we assume that it would be valid in the church?

Business does not expand into new areas without careful surveys and complete analysis of findings before a determination is made as to what it will market in a particular area. The findings determine inventory, advertising procedures, public relations programs, and the projected image that will best identify with those who must utilize the services or purchase the products. And as communities change, the inventory, advertising procedures, public relations programs, and projected image must be modified to accommodate those changes.

Local churches tend to view themselves as entirely different. In the world but not of the world. Wholly other to the fabric of humanity resulting from the warp and woof of community structure and being. Relating to God, it does not have to be concerned with mankind. Relating to the divine, it does not have to be concerned with the human. Relating to the heavenly, it does not have to concerned with the earthly.

This theological bent may have been appropriate in the Old Testament, but I find nothing to support it in the New Testament. There is nothing to indicate that it was consistent with Christ's teachings in the Gospels and nothing to support it as apostolic faith in the Epistles.

The Christian band was an exceptional group. They traveled. They preached. They contested traditions, priorities, and circumstances. And they gathered into their fellowship those who became participants in the way. The process has continued for almost 2000 years, and obviously twentieth-century Christians have not been as faithful to the task as those in the first century. Otherwise, the point of saturation in the world today would not be as far removed from the programmatic design of the churches as it is.

In our view of expanding programs, we have gone from one extreme to the other. We have gone from the participants in the gathered community to the persons most remote from the church's program. And we have not given consideration to still another significant group. These are the members of the particular church who are not involved. Perhaps we might refer to them as the dropouts. Those who seldom drop in. Or those who have never truly dropped in. Those who have never become a truly significant part of the program and life of the church. Why? What happened? How do folk become involved to the degree that they will go through the process of becoming participants without actually becoming significantly involved?

Certainly the dropouts must carry some of the blame. But the organization cannot remain blameless. The fault actually lies in the program dimension itself. Needs must be met. While there may have been a good relationship at the beginning, something went wrong. If they were in touch when joining the group, certainly they are not a significant part of the group now.

INTEGRATING PARTICIPANTS
AND SUSTAINING INTEREST

Let us consider three aspects to the process of integrating individuals into the program and sustaining the significance of their act. Here is perhaps the greatest weakness in organizational structure today. It is simple to join organizations today. Recently I read of a person who had more than 800 different credit cards. While that may be some kind of a record, it would not be difficult in our society for someone to unite with more than 800 groups or organizations. Most would require no financial commitment. Some would have no requirements at all. Just attend a meeting or fill out a form. While in some cases there would be some requirements for attending one or two events, many would not require even that.

Now it is true that meetings and training events will not automatically achieve the building of sound relationships. But they should at least give some understanding as to whether such a relationship should be established. In far too many instances, however, this has not been their purpose. The purpose was to join. Through the process one would become a member. When one makes the decision to progress to this stage, one is really already in. In the world of business, there are probationary periods, trial runs, or limited memberships of thirty, sixty, or ninety days.

This exposure period should be a time for determining whether the organization is interested in the candidate and whether the candidate is truly interested in the organization. The church suffers from the fact that many who hold membership do not actually belong and that many who should come into the membership will never belong because of the projected image of the church as an institution that is not relevant, not vital, and not important to the lives of people.

When a determination is made that there is a common interest, dedication to like goals, and an assurance that the personal and organizational resolve is enhanced, then membership should become a reality. This should certainly not happen before these can be determined beyond the shadow of a doubt.

Those uniting with an organization must be integrated

into the organization. Integrated and involved. This is not difficult if in the membership process one can discern that there is like interest and that both the organization and the individual can expand their interest and devote their energies to complementary goals. The institution will be more than anxious for the new member to become involved in order that it may extend and expand its program. The individual will be interested since the organization provides not only the beachhead against which his or her ideas can be tested but also the means of adding a dimension of corporate strength to his or her individual witness.

So often in organizational structures we tend to raise the question as to what an individual may or may not do for the organization. Seldom do we consider what the individual may do through the organization. You see, there is a vast difference. IBM Corporation's personnel policies list this as of supreme importance to the recruiting process. We tend to think of an organization for an organization's sake. Little wonder that there are so many dead churches and stagnant organizations. Rather, the importance of organizational structures should be the opportunity they provide to individuals to extend their lives, their services, their hopes, and their dreams.

Persons become interested in organizational life when their relationship is so keen that it is impossible to separate the goals and objectives of the individuals from the goals and objectives of the institution. Organizations ought to be the orchestration of individual endeavors. When the organization orchestrates the gifts, capabilities, and the activities of the individuals sharing in the enterprise, the organization becomes a powerful instrument and a significant institution.

There must then be a uniting of individual and organizational strength, and there must be integration of individual and group participation in the process.

Those uniting with a group must share common goals. Individual participation must not only orchestrate the activities and interests of those participating in the organization's life but focus on common goals. Actually, as membership expands and individuals enter the union and become integrated in the process, the goals and objectives are certain to need modification. In some cases the direction may change radically, though change is usually moderate. However, if it does not change at all, the organization cannot be benefiting from individuals' becoming parts of the process as fully as they might. Likewise, as individuals separate from the organization's life through alienation, moving, illness, or death, there will also be change. A certain influence, interest, and support will be lost. However, as such events are experienced, one will discover at times that enthusiasm increases and that commitment deepens as one individual dies or suffers a severe blow and others seek to compensate for the loss or take on new incentive as a tribute to the torch that may have been dimmed by circumstances.

Programs expand the mission of the church and its agencies as individuals become a part of the organizational life and work and an integral part of that life and work. Organizations expand programs to accommodate the interests, concerns, and capabilities of those who unite with them. When these interests and concerns are met, there are no limits to what the organization may do. The only limit will be that assumed by participants as a result of indifference, rejection, or curtailment of initiative and action.

10

Developing Staff

If you were to describe in a brief phrase the condition of the church today regarding staff, what would you say? I would have to put it in these terms: The wrong people doing the right things inadequately. Or the right people doing the wrong things imperfectly.

As a brief case study, take a staff person in your local situation and list in one column all the things that that person does, or for that matter, is expected to do. Beside it place a column in which to check the appropriateness of the task or function to that office. In a third column one would be required to check those tasks or functions that are not appropriate to the office. What is the result? The vast majority of the checks will be placed in the third column. There will be fewer checks in column two than in column three.

While this may be true in many other organizations, and possibly to some degree in the business world, it is certainly characteristic of the church today. It is responsible for the disintegration of professionalism in the church and for the difficulty of recruiting qualified persons for church vocations in our society today. I suppose one of the important reasons for this is that we tend to develop staff and program rather than program and staff.

Theological seminaries are considered the technical schools or educational facilities for preparing folk for church vocations. Little wonder that they have been so long in offering a bachelor's degree, or a diploma for graduate study. Study the curricula. Discern the expertise developed through theological training today.

There are far too many seminary graduates who say, "Here I am with a seminary degree, and my education qualifies me for nothing." Usually they assume that they are prepared for a vocation in the church. What vocation would you suggest? Ministry? Most graduates have not been trained even to conduct a funeral service or a wedding ceremony. Christian education? Certainly not without more training. Institutional chaplaincy? Those recruiting such personnel are not looking to recent graduates. The local church? Well, as long as small churches need ministers and ministers need work, there are some limited opportunities. More for men than for women. The church knows that it is employing an amateur and plans for on-the-job training. The minister knows that he or she is not adequately prepared and accepts a post with a limited salary because it offers on-the-job training as an additional benefit. After all, he or she is just *beginning* professional training.

In conferences across the country, I have stated that I learned everything in seminary except how to run a church. My oldest son, one generation removed from me, can make the same statement. The statement is never made to less than vigorous applause. Groups may differ with some statements I make, but this statement, above all, receives universal concurrence.

This is an issue that our denominations, and especially the theological seminaries, need to deal with. But seldom do I find persons in responsible positions really concerned. Middle judicatory leadership seems to be concerned, but the theologians and the denominational leadership are not attentive to their voices.

At best, then, those who are called to give leadership to

the church, and especially to our local churches, do not fill the bill. Servants? Certainly. Dedicated? I hope so. Hopeful? Without a doubt. Scared? There is no question about that at all.

We cannot solve this problem with this book, and stating the fact in this chapter probably will not make a great deal of difference. But it does give one an understanding of where we need to begin in our consideration of the task of developing staff in the church today.

Let us consider ten aspects of the task that are normal in the field of business and that must be norms for developing staff in the local church and related agencies as well:

Defining the task. This may be the most important assignment we face as we consider organizational life and work, but it is the one aspect that is likely to be overlooked or at least oversimplified.

As an example: A committee is elected to select and nominate a new pastor. What do they look for? What opportunities can they provide to a new leader? What is the pastor expected to do? What challenges will confront him or her? How long will it take the congregation, in defining goals, to attain the objective of this type of leadership?

But these questions are not usually raised when a committee seeks pastoral leadership. The committee tends to think of preaching, pastoral calling, and conducting the various meetings that any particular denominational form of government requires. The members of the committee view the situation in which the candidate serves and assume that if that person were to assume the role of pastoral leadership in their church, the situation would be comparable in a period of time.

Obviously we are not apt to have great success in selecting leadership as long as the nominating and selecting process is conducted by persons who are not trained or qualified for the task. In business those who engage in the selection process are as professional in their task as those they select for particular positions in the organization. If committee members were to take four fifths of the amount of time they expect to spend in the task of selecting the nominee for the pastoral office for the purpose of defining the task the nominee is to assume, there would be much more credibility to the process. There is little hope in the process until this is done.

Define the task. What is the work that needs to be done? What is the capability of the organization to meet the objective? What are the causes? What is the time frame? When accomplished, what will be the next step?

Define the task.

Here we assume that there is only one task to be done. Now we need to face the fact that when we define the task we are not speaking of an individual's responsibility but of the responsibility of an organization. What is the task of the organization? What must it do? You see, when we come to the point of selecting personnel, we may not be thinking of a single person. One has no idea of personnel, or of personnel needs, until one has defined the task.

In the area of the local church, what is the task? In terms of worship? In terms of education? In terms of evangelism? In terms of growth? In terms of present facilities? In terms of new facilities? In terms of existing programs? In terms of new programs? In terms of community? In terms of the denomination? In terms of ecumenical relations? In terms of racial, ethnic, and/or national groups? In terms of the aged? In terms of youth? In terms of those at life's prime? We could go on, and on, and on.

When the task, from the organization's point of view, is defined, we are in a position to move to the next step.

Determining the need. The word *need* takes on a double meaning at this point. The term could well apply to the need of the organization to fulfill its purpose. However, since we are directing our attention to the selection of staff, we are, of necessity, forced to consider the organization's need in terms of personnel, leadership, and/or expertise.

We faced the question, first, What is the organization's task? Now we face the question of what the organization needs in leadership to meet the demands that the task requires.

Obviously the needs will be legion. Considering that fact, we simply must come to the place where we can weigh the various needs, place them in sequence in light of priorities, and give prime consideration to those that are close at hand.

Here one needs to consider whether the priorities as seen by the select nominating group are consistent with the priorities of the total organization. If they are not, the personnel selection process will not be effective. That the needs of a select group within a parish can be met is no reason to assume that the needs of the total group may be met. Here those in the selecting process must ever be mindful of the fact that they are a representative group and that their primary responsibility is to represent the larger group that has delegated the task to them.

Matching persons with tasks is not simple. For the task is not just to match people with responsibilities but rather to determine the qualifications required of persons to do the tasks. The selecting of particular persons does not begin until we have actually defined the qualifications of the person to be considered for particular tasks, the meeting of particular needs.

What are the qualifications required of persons considered for particular tasks? From the standpoint of education? Experience? Expertise? Energy?

Viewing these few qualifications, we are suddenly aware that the needs of the organization need be defined, placed in sequence in terms of priorities, and programmed in units of need that are related and truly belonging to each other. In defining needs, we discover that the more completely they are defined, the more restrictive the task. In all likelihood, as we consider each of the needs, the organization will not be in a position to employ a specialist in meeting each need but will tend to seek a generalist with special capability in the area of several limited needs.

Here one must be mindful that the church is quite a different organization from the ordinary business institution. In the church the patrons are the directors and often serve as voluntary staff. The organization is broad and the marketing group ranges from the cradle to the grave. There are fewer limitations in church vocations than in any other discipline. Hence, the task of selecting leaders is much more difficult.

Here the selecting group will be required to program needs in terms of importance, significance, and utility within the body politic and of the urgency with which the selection process must take place in the light of these determining factors.

Considering that generalists rather than specialists will be required in most situations and that the generalists will have significant and special expertise in particular areas, it is then necessary in the selecting process to recognize that time frames must be established for certain functions and responsibilities and that a person's particular talents, gifts, expertise, and professional proficiency will likely be required for a particular period of time. This does not mean for a period of six months, a year, or two years. But we are likely to eliminate most, if not all, persons for consideration for a post for a period exceeding five years.

Those in the selecting process, then, should be in a position to suggest the time frame as a guide to an individual's consideration of a task and the organization's demand for services in terms of the professional qualifications of the candidate or nominee. Now it is certain that some objectives will not take five years to reach and that other objectives will require much more time. But we cannot expect expert leadership over an extended period if the goals are to be changed from time to time without matching objectives and expertise.

Having then defined the task and determined the need, we are prepared for the next step.

Surveying the resources. There are numerous resources in terms of equipment, facilities, and plant. Are the physical, real properties sufficient to meet the need in terms of personnel and program?

If not, when will they be available and what will be required of personnel to cause them to be available? If they are not to be available, how reasonable is the goal in the light of those limited resources? Often personnel are placed in an impossible situation simply because the necessary resources are never to be available to them.

Financial resources are of great importance, for if the particular resources considered above are not available or not adequate, it is possible that they might be obtained if the financial wherewithal were available to secure them. Are there financial resources to do the task at hand? Little can be done without money. Money is essential to every program as we consider facilities, equipment, buildings, materials, supplies, and, of course, personnel. We may very well accomplish our purposes without volunteers, but we cannot accomplish our purposes without those things that individuals must have to be effective in the functions to which they are assigned.

It is not unusual in the church today to minimize the need for financial resources in relation to the other needs evident in the organization's life and work. However, as we define the organization's need, it will generally become apparent that such an attitude is unwise, and indeed impossible.

To understand the financial needs related to the organizational need, as well as the task, it is essential that they, too, be placed in a time frame as well. What are the immediate financial needs? What are the financial requirements over the short term? What are the financial requirements over the long haul?

Certainly the financial resources over the long haul are

not usually available at the beginning of the process. Hopefully there will be seed money or start-up funding. Likely the objective to which the organization and leadership give themselves is to provide fiscal integrity to the process.

I am thoroughly convinced that there is nothing in the world that cannot be funded. This does not mean that everything can be funded as of yesterday or today—or even tomorrow. But it is possible to bring together financial needs and financial resources to accomplish programs, given the time and supporting services required to do so.

As the program evolves, it is expedient and necessary that adequate financial resources be available in the process.

Having defined the task, determined the need, and surveyed the various resources, we are ready for the next step.

Projecting progress and growth. Projecting progress and growth is important to every aspect of organizational life and work. It is important in terms of the goals that the organization has established. It is important in terms of the goals that leaders established as they relate to the organization. And it is important to individuals participating in the organization, for when progress and growth are not perceived, the interest of the group disintegrates and fails.

The absence of the profit motive makes it more difficult to define progress or specify goals that must be reached for the health of an organization's life. Nevertheless, standards must be established and measures defined to determine the effectiveness of leadership and the validity of the direction of program and/or service.

I suppose that we might more properly refer to this as goal setting, for certainly goals must be set and milestones for measuring progress defined along the way.

Assuming a course of action, how soon can we discern progress? What will the effect be in ninety days, six months, a year, five years?

Growth need not be measured as something that can be identified in numbers, distance, or time, but it must be an evidence discernible to those evaluating the progress and those related to the process. At times growth will be difficult to define. Nevertheless, it is essential that it be defined if there is to be reasonable expectancy in terms of the organization and a sense of attaining purpose in terms of the leadership.

When indices for growth are not defined and clearly understood by those assigning and assuming responsibility, there can be nothing but trouble in the organization.

Having defined growth or progress, together with the preceding three considerations, we are faced with a key element in our organizational structure.

Considering the options for leadership. When we began the chapter, it appeared that we had a simple task—employing someone to do a job. Well, it is just not that simple.

When we view personnel and personnel needs, we need to discern what options are before us in organizational life and work. Options? What do we mean by options?

There should be options in selection of personnel across denominational lines. The world of religion suffers because there is not the cross-fertilization of staff migration that we find in the world of business. There moves from IBM to General Electric to Xerox are common. Seldom are there moves from Episcopal to Methodist to Presbyterian. Doors need to be opened here.

But there are options in terms of the skilled and the general professional type within the denominational structures. We spoke of this earlier and indicated that in the church there well may be greater need for generalists who can give special attention to several areas of concern than for a specialist whose entire capability will relate to a single task.

But the selection process is not as simple as selecting between the specialist and the generalist in terms of the professional leadership. Many times consideration should center on a paraprofessional to serve in an agency to complement the services of the professional, either because the particular task does not require a professional or because the resources are not available to employ professional staff.

Even the classification of the paraprofessional may be too limiting when we consider the church. Often consideration needs to be given the nonprofessional. This is not really too farfetched for the religious organization, since we have already conceded that the professionally qualified leadership in the church is not really professionally qualified at all.

In the religious organization we must consider the volunteers. The church is a voluntary organization. The local church is a part of the network of voluntary leadership that circles the globe.

When we realize the limited resources available to the religious organization, we are mindful of the place and responsibility of volunteers in the total organizational structure.

In selecting staff, whether skilled or general, professional or paraprofessional, nonprofessional or volunteer, we need to insist that all be under a contractual arrangement if the process of leadership and program are to be well met. This must be done if for no other reason than to have in the contract a termination clause. Many organizations are strapped to death because they are firmly held to persons whom they cannot terminate. However difficult the process is as a result of organized labor, it could never be as difficult as in the voluntary organization.

We should not assume that volunteers cannot be professional or paraprofessional people. Simply because there is not a financial arrangement between the organization and the individual does not mean that professional services cannot be available at limited, or no, cost. In each event, however, the providers must be responsible to staff and the staff must be responsible for orchestrating these services.

The options for leadership then include professional, paraprofessional, and nonskilled persons, any of which may be salaried or volunteer.

Selecting staff. Considering the options weighed against the requirements of the agency, we are now in a position to actually select the persons to assume responsibility for staffing the organization.

In selecting staff, we should, again, be mindful of the time frame. Certainly some staff persons will occupy such a role in the organization's life and work that their services should be considered for a long term. Those, however, who may well make the greatest contribution to the organization's life and work may be those of very limited tenure. In religion we have given little consideration to positions of limited tenure—that of consultant, for example. And the church suffers from its failure to make use of such persons.

There are certain developmental processes that must be done, that must be done well and in a very limited period of time. In fact, many services can be of significance only at particular periods of time. Selection must be made for expertise at those particular periods of time.

We would do well to chart an organization's staff needs at particular periods of a projected future. Setting them up at three- or six-month intervals over a period of five years, one could well see the staff needs at particular points in the organizational progress and process and be in a position to make valid judgments concerning them from time to time.

At no time will an organization be in a position to have all the staff it would like to have. There are limits because of financial resources, limits because of organizational structure, limits because of time and circumstances, and sometimes limits because of location. Because of these limiting factors it is important that wise decisions be made to provide the best staffing possible for the most effective organizational structure.

In selecting staff, there are three types of positions to be considered.

ADMINISTRATION. Administrators should be selected on the basis of general or particular administrative skills governed by the resources of the agency and the number of employees. When administrative responsibilities lodge in a single staff person, the individual selected must be capable of meeting the administrative needs of the organization. Certainly he or she must be a person of diversified skills. He or she may be dealing with finance, personnel, purchasing, and the overall administrating of the program. The selecting process for this type staff person must calculate those areas where strengths are most important and where weaknesses will not cause the organization to suffer overly much. A number of things will govern this selection process.

The capability of the person serving in the particular position previously will be an important factor. It is not likely that two persons serving the same office in successive terms would excel in the same areas. Actually the successor's strength should be an area other than that of the preceding administrator. The organization should be able to ride for some time on the strength of the structure resulting from its unique situation.

More important are the capabilities of the person under consideration for the assignment. What distinct contribution is he or she capable of making in the short term? The long term?

Considering the contribution of the previous administrator and the present status of the organization, those selecting must determine the greatest needs at the present time. When all these considerations are applied to the selection process, the most likely candidate will emerge in a rather short time.

PROGRAM. As important as administrative staff is, those persons who serve in the program area are of supreme importance. The purpose of the church, agency, or organization is to accomplish the task for which it has been constituted, and that is best described as program. There are times that the program person is also the administrator. Here there must be an evaluation made as to which area—administration or program—is most important at the particular time. If administration has been the strength of the preceding staff person, program should be of primary importance now. If program has been the strength of the preceding staff person, administration may well be of primary importance now. This will depend, of course, on the priorities that the selection committee defines and the situation in the agency or organization from the standpoint of administration and program.

In the sermon "No Transplants Here," contained in my book *Developing Dynamic Stewardship*, I emphasize the fact that it is not possible to move conditions and situations from one location to another simply by moving staff. A program person may move from one agency to another, but the particular program in the preceding agency does not come with the person. Programs emerge from constituency, capability, and need in each particular agency. Those programs that emerge readily and successfully in one situation may simply fail in another situation.

The types of persons to be selected in the program area will be determined largely by the number of persons to be employed in that area. As in administration, if only one person is to be employed and there are a number of programmatic areas, then the person should be a generalist. If, however, numerous persons are to be employed, each will be selected in terms of the particular program area in which he or she is to carry responsibility.

There is unlikely to be a single program area so restricted, limited, and defined that a single capability will emerge. In the selection process the talents and capabilities of persons will move from one program emphasis to another as areas of previous strength progress on past momentum and areas of previous weakness emerge to proper strength with proper leadership in the program structure.

SUPPORTING STAFF. In administration as well as in program there is need for supporting staff persons. These may include the secretaries, bookkeepers, file clerks, and custodial staff. Some may wonder why we have not placed a property and maintenance staff between program staff and supporting staff—engineers, custodians, janitors, etc. In my thinking, such persons should be looked upon as program people. Building is for program. Restoration is for program. Maintenance is for program. And in some cases there is a danger when these factors move in the direction of administration, for in a real sense of the word they administrate, or govern, the things that an agency may do. These persons should not occupy such a role.

In selecting the title for this third category of staffing, I have used the word *supporting* rather than *subordinate* staff. Subordinate staff members assume that their primary function is to be subordinate to other staff persons. Supporting staff are mindful that they are in supporting roles to the administrative and program responsibilities. This is most important. In a very real sense of the word, every staff member must be in a supportive role, or the administrative and program processes will be chaotic.

In considering the administrative, program, and supporting staff, it is important to establish a time line and determine the staffing needs at intervals across the organization's life. Previously we suggested that such time lines be at three-month intervals. If this is done, and there are limited resources and staff, there are likely to be more numerous short-term, or temporary, staffing positions and more mobility among staff persons.

In *Models for Ministry* I explain at length the value of sharing staff among churches and agencies for the greatest utilization of capabilities and resources. Consider these offices and functions:

Christian education directors: preschool and kindergarten; elementary education; junior high and senior high; young adult, adult, and senior adult groupings.

Music directors: choral and instrumental.

Office workers: secretary, typist, bookkeeper, accountant, file clerk, word processing staff, library and data bank assistant.

Maintenance workers: interior and exterior custodial services, carpenter work, painting and decorating, lawn care, heating and air conditioning, equipment and supplies, purchasing and quantity control.

Counselors: particular age groups, exceptional persons, problem types, career development and life planning.

Educators: age groups, Bible and theology, morals and ethics, service and outreach.

Numerous persons with expertise in these areas could serve the ministry and mission of a half dozen churches and agencies effectively and well—and economically.

We see this process at work in staffing a few organizations today. The trend will become more obvious with dollars decreasing in value and greater competition for excellence in personal services.

Certainly this is a proper course for staffing religious organizations today.

Assigning responsibility. As important as the process of selecting staff is, the task of assigning responsibility is of supreme importance. It is seldom that one can build a good staff unless each person carries responsibilities that are clearly defined, is considered capable of doing his or her work, and has an opportunity to be creative in his or her own field. People discern the importance of a position in terms of the responsibility they assume, and if that responsibility is not crystal clear, the person will have no sense of challenge, direction, or accomplishment. Each position must be reasonable and responsible.

While we tend to place positions into either administration or program, there are many positions that fall into the areas between the two. And this is not a problem when we recognize that all persons are supporting staff, even when carrying major responsibility in administration or program. Each staff person must be supportive of all other staff persons. But each staff person must have a responsibility peculiar to his or her particular office. In a sense, then, all staff persons are supportive of each other, and in particular areas rely on certain staff members for particular things.

St. Paul illustrates the effectiveness of the church as a body. Each individual is a part of the body, as an arm, a leg, an eye, a tooth. His illustration should prove helpful to an understanding of this factor in organizational life and work and assist us to more meaningful organizational structures today.

Who determines responsibility? The matrix emerges from the board of directors. They may, and usually will, delegate responsibility to particular staff positions, but this does not relieve the board of the responsibility of making sure that the organization is properly structured for maximum service. In most situations the senior administrator and the senior program person will determine the responsibilities for those in their respective areas. And in many cases the responsibilities of staff members will be defined through a consultation process between those in administration and those in program, since it frequently happens that positions are not as clearly defined in one area as in the other. Each position will relate to program and each position to the administrative processes.

Structuring accountability. We would tend to assume that accountability will coincide with responsibility; that is, those that determine responsibility are those to whom accountability is given. While this is true in many situations, it is not true in all. For as responsibilities are assigned, so also are the guidelines for accountability, and often accountability is to someone other than those who define responsibility.

There is schism and disunity in many organizations because these two matters are not crystal clear and some assume that accountability is to those who have defined responsibility when it is not. That senior administrators and program officers know the accountability structure does not mean that persons sharing in program and administration know, and unless it is clearly defined and clearly understood, there is a lack both of communication and consolidation of effort.

In both accountability and responsibility the time factor is important. There are times when each staff person has full responsibility and is accountable for all matters. There are other times when the responsibility and accountability are contingent on time or on other persons. This must be understood by those in both supervisory and supporting capacities.

While the degree of responsibility and accountability will vary in terms of hours and days on duty and the times when one is not on duty, there are responsibilities and accountabilities that prevail regardless of the circumstances. In these cases certain responsibilities and accountabilities are delegated. These too must be clearly defined and known throughout the organizational structure. To ensure credibility in positions at all times, it is not only expedient but necessary that these responsibilities and accountabilities be matters of record before the fact rather than after the fact. After the fact there are always evidences of evading issues and persons protecting themselves and their positions when things go wrong. Certainly everything will not be right all the time.

The reporting process is important not only in determining the person-to-person linkage but in determining the means and time for reporting. Unless these are scheduled, there is a tendency to make matters fragmented, and the only time matters come into focus is when they are not proper, or out of order, rather than when they are proceeding properly in an organization's life. In many situations there is a tendency, when things are going well, to say, "No report." This ought not be. "No news is good news" is a reasonable saying, but it is not a responsible statement. Reports and reporting processes should be scheduled and should verify the positive as well as the negative. When merit increases or promotions are under consideration, reasonable input should be available to the negotiator from the responsibility, accountability, and reporting processes.

Measuring effectiveness. This is one of the most difficult tasks in interpersonal relations, and in order that the process be fair, it is especially important that the responsibility and accountability factors be perfectly clear. For how does one measure effectiveness if there are different standards by which individuals or groups measure effectiveness?

Time lines are important in measuring effectiveness as well, and the time lines must be reasonably spread to accommodate fair results. In organizational life we tend to expect too much too soon. Usually a church or agency will do well to go to an objective source outside the organization to establish guidelines for measuring performance. Those involved in the administrative and program functions are too close to the situation to make valid appraisals.

In measuring effectiveness, there are not only the factors that relate to a position (or responsibility) and time but the factors that relate to individual differences as well. No two persons will perform the same function in identical ways. Individuals set their pace, exercise their ability, direct their interest, and prioritize in their own unique ways. And because priorities, interests, and capabilities vary from time to time, there is no perfect matrix for measuring effectiveness.

Effectiveness needs to be measured in terms of tasks, responsibilities, and time, and effectiveness needs to be measured with compassion and understanding. Many affirm that there is more compassion (or "heart") in the world of business than in the world of religion. Very likely this is the result of the fact that measures are more readily defined in business than in religion. In religion many are making assessments based on different standards. At times individuals will seem more effective than at other times, but strange as it may seem, often a person's effectiveness is greater when the measurements indicate least effectiveness. In measuring effectiveness, we tend to use measures that are too limited to give full consideration to programs, persons, and needs.

No one will be effective in all areas of his or her responsibility, and here, too, leadership needs to determine the priorities to be computed in measuring effectiveness. Those priorities and standards also must be known by all those engaged in the process before the fact as well.

Providing remuneration. The matter of rewards, or remuneration, is a subject of its very own and will be considered in detail in the next chapter.

11

Funding Staff

In the local churches, as well as in voluntary organizations in the nonprofit sector, the laborer is not considered worthy of his or her hire. Support in kind has been an accepted component of remuneration, and dedication to cause and mission a complement to the task. Few, if any, are adequately paid, and little attempt has been made to provide wage scales, fringe benefits, and working conditions equal to those in the business and professional world. There are several important reasons:

1. Collective bargaining is not a force in church vocations. Individuals have been left to bargain for themselves. And in most cases where there has been a meeting on salaries and fringe benefits, those representing the organization have not been knowledgeable in these areas. For some, the remuneration provided to the clergy and lay employees has exceeded the personal income of the representatives themselves, and they have not been discerning of the needs, or the rewards, that should be met for the professional and paraprofessional persons.

2. In the church and church-related fields, there are few job descriptions that adequately reflect the education,

experience, and expectations of the employee. And even when these descriptions do exist, no value is placed upon them. Education and experience figure strongly in the field of education, but they are without tables or standards in organized religion.

3. There is an assumption that church and church-related vocations are of divine calling and that the rewards should be other than monetary and/or material. Just deserts will be forthcoming at the end of time. The primary reward is assumed to be that of doing the will of God.

Organized religion needs to address itself to this issue, but it is not likely to do so soon. Female students are nearing a majority in the theological seminaries. Women generally receive less in salaries and fringe benefits than men do. With a preponderance of female clergy, there will be little or no pressure to increase levels of remuneration for another decade or two. Equal rights is a boon to cheap labor in religion.

Somewhere the church needs to begin to consider not only the problem but the course that needs to be followed in the future. This would almost lead me to a fourth reason as to why church-related remuneration is so low: a misunderstanding of Jesus.

I was raised to believe that "my Master was so very poor." He had "no place to lay his head." He was a wandering teacher without standing and seemingly without a portfolio.

Recall the fact that Jesus was born in a stable not because the Holy Family was not a family of means, but because the hotel was lacking in facilities. There was, in fact, no room.

When it was time to pay taxes, Jesus did not say, "We have no money; we are clergy; we must be exempt." He sent his disciples fishing, and they paid their tax in full.

Even at Calvary, where the outcast of the ages was to hang on a tree, his robe was considered of so great a worth that those who bargained for it would not tear the cloth.

Jesus was born into a family of means. He was wrapped in swaddling clothes, a practice of the elite. His family were people of substance. His being and carriage was such that when he came into the villages and cities, he was entertained in the very best of homes. The inauguration of the Last Supper was in a chamber of affluence. When he died, his body was placed in a significant tomb.

The idea that those who serve God should be self-denying and self-defaming is one of the strange tricks of history, and the only persons who have been well cared for have been the popes and the bishops. Perhaps the clergy have not been self-assertive. Perhaps the laity have not been convinced that the clergy are entitled to reasonable and proper support. However, the clergy, in misunderstanding economic facts relating to the life of our Lord, and the laity, by being willing to abide with this misunderstanding and interpretation, have locked the clergy into a state of economic disadvantage that is a shame to the Gospel.

Henry Ford believed in the five-dollar day and transformed American industry. It is unfortunate that at that moment in history there was not someone who believed in the twenty-five-dollar sermon. Organized religion has never had a champion for economic justice.

Because the leadership in the church has been grossly underpaid, every person in church and church-related vocations is underpaid. The salary schedule is governed by remuneration of the clergy, and no professional group is as seriously underpaid when one considers education, experience, and work load. Compare the salaries of every professional, paraprofessional, skilled, and unskilled worker in the church and church-related agencies, and you will see that the remuneration is considerably less than in service to other organizations and agencies. If you compute the fringe benefits, the salary package is even worse.

Imagine the attitude of the world of business and commerce when the church advocates fair wages, fringe benefits, and better working conditions. Yet the church, from denominational leaders and ecumenical officers to local pastors and activist groups, has been very free to give its advice, and resolution after resolution has fallen on deaf ears simply because the church does not practice what it preaches in the economic support it provides for those who serve in its vocational roles.

How can the church resolve the situation? Where can it begin? What guidelines should it use?

Some efforts are being made, but they all begin at the wrong place. Generally they begin with a comparison with what other denominations and churches are paying or they begin with a comparison with other occupations that themselves have been depressed under the influence of the church, i.e., private educational institutions and nonprofit agencies.

All these vocations are seriously underpaid because they have their roots in organized religion, where service was considered to be humanitarian, philanthropic, and charitable. All in such vocations are to have their eyes on service and not on their pocketbooks, and the reward for service is to be the satisfaction of doing good works and not the satisfaction of being fairly rewarded for one's work.

Where should we begin? We must begin at the very top. The key person in the church's organization or institution's life and work is the pastor.

REMUNERATION FOR CLERGY

What guidelines shall we use for their remuneration?

Some suggest that we structure a salary schedule that would equal the income of the doctors, dentists, lawyers, and school *teachers*. Notice the italics for those in education. Not the school administrators—superintendents and principals—but the school teachers.

As a guideline the pastor should be in the top 5 percent of those with earned incomes in the parish. Unless he or she is in that economic bracket, effective ministering to those in the upper 25 percent in income in the local church will be difficult.

Through the years there has been a polite and somewhat

condescending look at the clergy among those in the upper economic echelons. They have not taken the clergy seriously. Problems that should, and could, ordinarily be handled by the clergy have gone to the psychiatrist and psychologist. And in cases when the spiritual counsel would be most important, the private counselor has not provided the spiritual help that the individual has needed inasmuch as he or she has not been schooled in theology and his or her orientation has not been in the spiritual arena. The church has been without credibility for many because it has not provided the economic orientation that has given the standing and stature the spiritual leader has required to perform his or her mission.

If Jesus had had the economic status most assume him to have had, and if he had been the mere wandering poet, orator, and magician he is often portrayed to have been, he would never have established the Christ-event in history. He became the turning point in history and began the Christian Era because his stature was complementary to the task given to him by God.

Let us begin, then, by providing the clergy with salaries equal to a level in the top earned-income brackets of the parish members.

REMUNERATION FOR
ADMINISTRATIVE STAFF

Administrative staff members have always been at a disadvantage because of the limited salary scales established by the churches and church-related institutions and organizations for clergy. If those in the top positions in the religious organizations are not adequately paid, then those in every other position are penalized in the remunerative process.

For indices to salary scales for the administrative staff, let us assimilate the salary schedules of the top 10 percent of the business-industrial establishments in the given geographical area and establish salary schedules consistent with the remuneration of employees in that area.

Program persons should be among those for whom re-muneration is consistent with vice-presidents, executive directors, and departmental executives in the same selected corporations in the business-industrial complex. Not only should the scales be consistent, but the increments and the timing for increments should also be consistent with those types of schedules in the business world.

Now if these processes are to be instituted, there will have to be measures for performance and the means to de-termine the effectiveness of the particular employee. For-tunately there will be opportunity for greater movement between the ecclesiastical and business arenas when there is a consistency in standards, remuneration, and operation. Those who produce should be moved from positions of less productivity to positions of greater productivity. Those who do not produce should be removed from their positions. Organized religion cannot afford the luxury of inexperi-enced and inefficient personnel.

REMUNERATION FOR
SUPPORTING STAFF

When we move from the administrative staff to the sup-porting staff, we tend to draw a fine line. It is a difficult line to define because in the vast majority of our churches, there are few staff members, and the ability to place one in one classification and another in another classification is almost an impossibility.

Supporting staff will consist of those who receive their orders and instructions from those occupying the positions to which they are responsible. In the business-industrial complex you will find among them secretaries, typists, file clerks, receptionists, maintenance and repair persons, and the custodial staff. Remuneration for all of these must not only be consistent with the remuneration provided in the business-industrial arena but actually establish a pattern for others to follow. More perhaps; the same at least; but certainly no less.

In financial remuneration let us remember that in the pastoral circle the income should be consistent with the earned income of the top 5 percent in the local parish. All other staff persons should receive salaries consistent with those businesses and industries in the top 10 percent for the area.

Fringe benefits and working conditions are grossly inadequate for those who serve in church and church-related vocations. Some efforts have been made in the areas of pensions and medical and surgical care. However, programs giving special consideration for prescribed medicines, eyeglasses, and dental care are almost foreign to those in ecclesiastical services.

What indices may be used for those in church vocations? We have suggested that in terms of the salary or wage scale that the sum should equal that for similar positions in the top 10 percent of industrial-commercial enterprises in the area. Fringe benefits should also be consistent with the same.

Organized religion needs to set the example. It should not look to the world of business for a model. The world of business should look to the church for its model. In this sense the salary computation equal to the commercial-industrial complex in the top 10 percent should be a first step, and in time organized religion should not only be the model for fringe benefits but the model for the remuneration of employees itself.

The church: A model

—in salaries
—in disability income
—in health care
—in vacation and holiday-recreation opportunity
—in incentive for workmanship
—in retirement income

Now the first response to these suggested courses of action will surely be negative, because "organized religion cannot afford it." If the church is to be an agency of integrity, credibility, and influence, it has no alternative.

Some years ago one of the world's outstanding theologians declared that we were at the "beginning of the end of the Christian Era." His assumption was based on theology and the theological outlook of the church and the need for Christocentric theology in the world. I say that we are at the threshold of the beginning of vitality in the Christian Era as the church assumes a proper role in industrial-organizational life in this last quarter of the twentieth century.

Where will the funding come from? Obviously it will come from the constituency—a constituency that will respond with more than adequate support for organizations efficiently operated, adequately managed, and modularly structured to serve spiritual, social, and moral needs.

12

Meaningful Profiles
for Ministry
and Service

The family concept in the household of faith is not new. It is as old as the Fatherhood of God and the Brotherhood of Man. Our Savior was ushered into time in an identifiable family relationship at birth. A type of family relationship is evident in numerous communities from Nazareth to Bethany. And the current life-style of a rather significant number in our society who enjoy group living supports the family identification assured to the disciples of our Lord.

When individuals unite with a church, they enter into a covenant relationship with their Lord and the spiritual community in which, hopefully, they will have a part. We sometimes tend to think of this relationship as little more than having one's name on a membership roll and receiving a certificate identifying that relationship. Actually, those are the records of the event and not the event itself.

A covenant relationship is caring and sharing. It is living in loving concern for others and at the same time sensing loving concern for oneself. Sharing one's life, interests, activities, and possessions with others. Having the privilege of sharing life, interests, activities, and possessions belonging to others in areas of common interests and in achieving common purpose.

When we define this covenant relationship, we soon realize that this places most of us a long way from a meaningful relationship in our church affiliation today. In fact, the word *affiliation* denotes our actual relationship to the church and to its members more adequately than the current relationship we have described above. Many sense that there is little or no caring, or sharing, in the organization. They affiliate with a church and identify with its purposes and objectives with little more feeling and significance than casting a ballot for a candidate or party. In a sense, in uniting with a church, most do little more than cast a ballot for Jesus and register their vote for the church.

Little is accomplished by determining where the blame is to be placed. Rather, the question is, How can we cultivate a covenant relationship with the people of God? How can we develop a real sense of sharing and caring in the church today?

The key is relatedness.

RELATEDNESS

All persons must come to an understanding of their relationship to the household of faith and their place in the "family" structure.

Consider a family. There are many relationships in a family. There is the relationship of the spouses, the husband and wife. There are the relationships of the children. These will differ from time to time and from circumstance to circumstance. My wife and I have raised four children, and through the course of years, we have seen many changes. Activities, interests, behavior, and even capabilities vary with time and influence personal relationships. The boys are separated each by two years, and the girl is six years younger than the youngest boy. Place any two of them together and circumstances change. They are the same boys and the same girl. Place the girl with her oldest brother and you have one set of circumstances. Place her with the middle son and you have another set of circumstances. Place her with the youngest son and you have still another set of circumstances.

Pair off each of the boys in similar patterns and you discover circumstances varying from one to the other in vast dimensions.

Then consider the implications as you move from sets of two persons to sets of three, then the sets of four, five, and six. Add to each of these groupings one parent, then the other parent, and finally both parents. Vast differences, aren't there?

Bring into this scene the more distant relations. The grandparents and the grandchildren. The aunts and uncles. The cousins. The nieces and nephews. The result is a vast array of significant relationships with each unique unto itself and yet making a distinct contribution to the strength and potential of the whole family unit.

Carry this over into a local church and see how exciting it becomes as one is not limited to just two, four, or six persons, or to one, two, or three generations. Whether a church has twenty members or two thousand members, consider the scope, variety, significance, and potential of these relationships—especially when we conceive of them as closely knit.

Obviously these cannot all be one-to-one relationships. In the larger congregations there will be a limit to the number of these types of relationships for each individual. Marshall McLuhan believes that persons are unable to relate in a meaningful way to more than a hundred persons in any society. However valid you consider the thesis, it is obvious that there are not going to be significant relationships involving an entire congregation. Yet, it is important that meaningful relationships be developed in the local church situation.

The development of meaningful relationships requires organization for the cultivation of relationships, and the organization process requires documentation.

DOCUMENTATION

In earlier chapters we have emphasized the importance of discerning needs as well as developing an understanding of the capability and potential for ministry and mission in the local church or agency. In some cases these needs will be documented and in some cases they will not. Regardless of whether they are documented or not, they must be identified. Actually, an organization is not likely to do much about them unless they are documented.

There are a number of ways by which information may be gathered and documented.

Surveys. Many local churches and organizations provide each new member an extensive question-and-answer form for the purpose of gaining information concerning the individual's education, experience, interests, and needs. Age tells us some things, marital status tells us still other things, education is a key to certain capabilities, vocational and avocational experience provide still other indices, and past involvements in like situations give birth to prospective development in the future.

It is not enough to survey or document experience, vocation, interest, and past performance from those uniting with the church or organization. At least once every five years surveys need to be made of groups, members, and friends in order that programs may be structured on information that is both current and valid. The information gained from this feed-in should provide a profile of each person and family unit as well.

Individual and family profiles. Significant facts that should be included in the individual/family profile include program responsibilities and/or involvement, public information, and financial data.

Program responsibility and personal involvement will become valuable indices for organizational growth and development. Activities in worship, church school, women's work, men's work, youth work, and membership on the official boards and administrative bodies of various organizations should be noted. Past experience and involvement make possible a more reliable and effective selecting, nominating, electing, and appointing process as leadership is recruited, cultivated, and introduced. Reliable leadership will emerge from data banks containing experience and involvement.

Public information gleaned from newspapers, newsletters, and periodicals, as well as from other sources, should be included in the individual/family profile. Many times churches and voluntary agencies fail to learn of the expertise persons have that has not emerged through the organizational structure of the local church. It may be evident in service clubs, social groups, and community involvement. The cross-fertilization of ideas and experience makes for gain in the religious organization as well as in community organizations.

Many churches and local organizations will not be able to subscribe to clipping services. Input from print media is not difficult to develop. Volunteers, especially among the aged and confined, will enjoy serving the organization by scanning local sources, clipping relevant items, and placing information in the individual/family profiles. They can at least compile the information and submit it to a librarian or coordinator serving the process. Manila folders may be prepared for individuals with cross-indexing for family relationships. One retired man of eighty-six years in Denver coordinates the work of a dozen folk who are confined to their homes but who, by telephone and mail, have established a network for gathering information that is placed in individual/family folders twice each month. If there were no value to the process at all except for the importance it holds for the participants, it would be very worthwhile. A look at the organization and activities of their 3000-member church will easily convince one that the process works and is very much worthwhile.

Nominating and leadership-selection groups generally assume that they know the members, their experience, and capabilities. After profiles are developed, they soon discover how little they knew about people and the tremendous potential that has been lost simply because organizations have left too much to memory and to chance.

Financial data. Financial data in the individual profile should include:

Contributions.

Causes to which the individual gave.

Financial commitments.

Track record for payment.

Whether the individual owns his or her residence, business, or other property.

Whether the individual has been involved in the organization's programs for personal estate planning.

Whether the individual has a will.

Whether the individual has established a trust.

Previously we have stated that various organizations are neglectful in keeping adequate records of the various financial campaigns that have been conducted for the organization's benefit through the years. When the campaign and pay-up period is over, the records are destroyed. Each time an organization begins a new campaign, it practically starts from scratch.

If profiles are developed for individual members and used appropriately, there is opportunity for developing most effective processes utilizing the experience and potential groomed from the participating members and those members who will participate more fully when more adequate planning and development take place.

These values are evident as one looks to future financial campaigns. But one need not think only of financial campaigns to discover great value in the financial information stored in the individual profiles. Organizations are always in need of funds. Special concerns, unusual events, and unexpected shortfalls in funding needs are common and continuous. In many of these types of situations, the decision is to limit or abandon programs unless evident resources are at hand. Resources are more readily available when we bring together interests, financial potential, and funding needs. As I indicated earlier, there is nothing in the world that cannot be funded. The task is to bring the funding resources and the funding needs together.

Opportunities for special gifts, memorials, and gift annuities; for the development of charitable-remainder trusts; for grants of real estate and personal property; and for resources in bequested income resulting from personal estate planning have their potential in personal profiles. The profiles gain in significance and importance as they become instrumental in providing resources for ministry and mission.

Correspondence and reports. Through the years I have been impressed with the medical records that my physicians and surgeons have kept on me. As I have moved from city to city, the files have gone from one location to another, and each succeeding doctor has had access to the records developed during the whole of my medical history. Continually they are able to prescribe treatment and medication based on that history to date. This type of process is foreign to the church, even though clergy are professional people and their important mission is the care and cure of souls. A part of their professional task is not only to build upon particular history but also to keep proper records and sustain the process for the future.

Each pastor usually begins from scratch. He or she must depend largely on attitude, personal experience, and sometimes hearsay. And yet we consider it professional ministry, counseling, and care.

Copies of personal and professional correspondence should be placed in individual files. Incoming correspondence as well as copies of replies must be retained if intelligent service is to be provided to parishioners. Clergy are physicians with responsibility for spiritual health!

The record should include not only correspondence but also reports of call resulting from personal visits, and notes from counseling sessions and office visits involving the professional staff of the local church.

Such records are important—as important as the records of baptisms, confirmations, marriages, ordinations, and/or installations. They may be more important, in fact. They contain keys to understanding persons, interests, needs, priorities, goals, and therapeutic options and opportunities for spiritual growth and healthy souls.

These all go together to form profiles.

They may be a means of monitoring parish life.

They may be a means to concern, financial support, and service.

They will be a means to meaningful service to those who are indeed "seekers of the way."

13

Indices from the Past
to Assist Leadership
in the Future

After accepting the call to become the senior pastor of the Fifth Presbyterian Church in Springfield, Illinois, in 1952, I learned that I was the third "R. K." in succession to serve in that pastorate. When I left the pulpit in 1963, I was also the third "R. K." to have served for a period of eleven years. Over thirty-three years three "R. K.'s" had provided spiritual leadership to that congregation. Service began with the Reverend Robert S. Kieser, who during my ministry in Springfield served the Fourth Presbyterian Church. He was succeeded by the Reverend Roy A. Kale, who also resided in that same city and served as the Associate Director of the Illinois Council of Churches.

My two predecessors, because they were still holding portfolios in that very city, contributed much to my ministry there. Their friends in the congregation appreciated my consideration of them and, as a result, supported my leadership far better than they might have had I taken a negative attitude.

Many times I have been pained as I have heard clergy holding a disrespectful view speak unkindly of their predecessors.

The past is prologue to the future. Each pastor must accept as a foundation the work that has gone on before him or her, whether it appears to have been built on sand or stone. Certainly one will appreciate some aspects of preceding leadership more than others, and at times there will be a tendency to be critical of certain aspects of it. It is good to give the benefit of the doubt to those preceding you, however, for we do not always know all the facts or understand all the implications, and there are always personal factors that cannot be fully comprehended.

There is little that we can do about the past. We can build a better future by discerning those strengths that emerge from the past. And if there have been mistakes, let them too provide wisdom for the future.

We should consider especially five major indices from the past that can strengthen the future with an affirmative design.

INFORMATION

There is history that is unique to every congregation. Even if an organization is newly formed, there is considerable history that emerges from the developmental stages.

Biographical history. We learn most about the Bible through the people of the Bible. We learn much about organizations when we gain in our knowledge of the people in the organization's life and work. One may learn of the persons who shared in the organizational stages, those who pioneered to bring the project or agency into reality, and those who provided leadership through the formative years.

Much may be learned through biographical details that give clues to the type of person who will best relate to the organization, the capabilities that will be most appreciated, and the types of persons who simply could not be interested or involved in the program.

In organizational life there are the biographical details of individuals and the biographical details of families as well. There are usually more details of a biographical nature playing in the decision-making processes of a church or organization than many assume. And as in the church we believe that a parish should become a family of faith, we need to realize that many times the church is families exercising their faith.

Organizations with strong family roots do not tend to be open in the participation dimension. New families coming into the church need to be strong if they are to be identified, and they will never integrate into the group unless they become a significant presence. This type of institution continues to be family oriented and, while limited in size, will have a cluster of constituency that will keep the organization on a rather even keel year after year.

When there is an absence of individual family visibility, the organization tends to grow—and later to diminish—with rapidity. There is less stability. Its strength is in numbers, and it depends on laws of averages to sustain its mission and purpose.

The biographical details of leadership are important. In the local church we think of pastoral leadership. Here much may be learned by the types who have served. Where did they come from? Where did they go? Were they single? Did they have families? If they had families, how did they relate to the parish? Did family involvement cease when the pastoral leadership was terminated? What of their education? Experience? Theological orientation? Ability? What were their weaknesses and strengths? These are all important considerations, and one simply cannot know much about an organization's life and work if one does not know a great deal about those whose lives, blood, sweat, and tears entered into the fabric of its being.

Biographical information concerning the lay leadership is equally important. Who are the persons of stature in the organizational structure and history? What positions did they hold in the church or agency? What positions did they hold in secular life? What contributions did they make to the organization, the community, and to other agencies? What influence do these matters have on the organization today?

We have much to gain when we learn of the people whose lives and work are enmeshed in an organization's life. Timing, too, is important.

In the introduction to this chapter, I wrote of three "R. K.'s" serving the Fifth Presbyterian Church in Springfield, Illinois, for periods of eleven years each. This speaks well of an organization, and it speaks well of leadership, too.

We can learn much about an organization if we can determine the length of the pastorates and administrations, the length of service of lay leadership, and the length of membership participation. Carrying over from the organization into the community, we can measure the stability of membership inherent in an organization with the span of years that folk reside in a particular community. When individuals and families participate in an organization's life and work for only brief periods, but the residence in the community is of long duration, it reveals the fact that long-term needs have not been met. The desirable optimum is that the participating factors in the organization would be near equal to the residing factors in the community.

Geographical history. Geography enters into the history of organizations, and the very health of a parish or agency may result from the sins or blessings of mountains, rivers, forests, deserts, thoroughfares, and commercial and/or residential areas.

Geographical factors are not consistent. Features change with time. Highways, byways, and changes in community design and transportation are significant. Many churches are in locations difficult to reach. Parking areas are limited or nearly nonexistent. Public transportation is unavailable, inaccessible, or too costly for many, though the original site chosen seemed a prize location for all time.

The geographical history of the institution is important, and projections into the future will emerge from them.

Social history. How has the organization related to other organizations? The religious? The secular? The ecumenical? As individuals are known by the company they keep, churches and agencies are best understood by the associations they sustain. Those that relate well become the stronger churches and agencies. Those that do not relate well tend to become isolated and weak.

It is important to learn the history of the organization from the standpoint of the secular and ecumenical connections, and it is important to discern the connection in the denominational or political structure as well. This is true whether the particular church is in a connectional system or not. There are many Congregational churches that are "presbyterian" and there are many Presbyterian churches that are almost totally "congregational" in their ecclesiastical posture. Their orientation will govern administrative policy and program.

Economic history. This is not usually difficult to chart. Denominational journals, directories, and statistical reports provide much of this type of information, and they are available from the offices, as well as the archives, of the denomination.

The annual reports of the organization and of the various groups within the organization provide important information concerning the strength and direction of the institution. Much of this type of information is not submitted in reports to the denomination and, because of goals and assessments, is never included in a particular church's or agency's reports.

BENCHMARKS

Having become informed concerning the history of the organization, it is important that one discern the benchmarks in an organization's progress.

We have written of short- and long-range planning and

the importance of setting goals for both short-term and long-term objectives. This type of planning, though not always formal or known, is evident in the fabric of organizational history, and as one pieces together the development of the organization, individual accomplishments tend to fall into chapters representing levels of operation and/or periods of time. The attainment of such may well be interpreted as benchmarks in an organization's progress.

Benchmarks in an organization's progress are important for several reasons.

1. The impress of each benchmark is an indicator of the organization's strength and intent at a particular time. Benchmarks of this type will be evident in relocations, new buildings, additions to existing plants, or expansion of facilities and staff. Significant milestones in an organization's life confirm strength and dedication.

Strength and dedication in the past is indicative of a potential for the future. When great things have been done, great things may be done—and will be done.

2. The frequency of significant benchmarks indicates the vitality of the organization. The impress of the benchmark is important because of the size and stature of the project. Frequent such benchmarks spell a continuing strength, valor, and hope, and a sustained momentum and capability.

One ought look to the impress of such benchmarks and discern the reason for accomplishment. Certainly there will be evidences of leaders, drivers, and dissenters. Of families and groups, and circumstances and situations that may or may not be relevant to them. Of an unusual gift, a bequest, or a grant. One may find a trick of fate in which circumstances entirely outside the congregation made for blessing or catastrophe, for example, a new highway or unusual funding beyond a parish's ordinary capability.

Many communities have unusual church structures funded by families as memorials. The philanthropy of the single family measures far beyond the capability of an entire parish.

The reasons, or sources, are significant to measure more adequately the capability of an organization over the long haul. If I as a clergyperson were to choose a position of leadership in a particular situation, I would prefer that significant benchmarks be frequent—the product of an organization's life and the work that people do together. This product, too, must be measured with considerable care, for significant gifts, grants, and memorials are seldom provided to groups, organizations, or agencies that do not have credibility or integrity.

3. The effect of each benchmark on the organization's life and work is an important attitude indicator. Does the organization actually move forward and upward as a result of the significant indicators of progress or does it "rest on its oars" and experience a period of indifference and/or organizational decline?

Certainly there will be highs and lows in an organization's history. There will be plateaus of greatness and elevations of lesser importance. Benchmarks should form a staircase into the future wherein each benchmark provides a step onward and upward. The basic direction is significant. Such a staircase is indicative of significant levels of opportunity ahead.

The history and the benchmarks tend to bring out the strengths and weaknesses of the organization.

CHARACTER

Individuals have character and so do families and groups. As character differs from individual to individual, so it differs from family to family and from group to group. Character is an important factor in marriage and family life as well as in membership and participation.

Character does not tend to change. While we believe in conversion and reformation, they do not change character. Characteristics before conversion and reformation remain the same after conversion and reformation. The

character and characteristics that made Saul of Tarsus made
Paul the Apostle. The character and characteristics that
made Luther the Professor made Luther the Protestant.

Character that emerges from an organization's past will
project into the future. This is an unavoidable fact of history, and whether we deal with the biographical data from
individuals or the annals of organizational life, the character
is established and will be fixed for the future.

Incompatibility with organizational structure and design
should be avoided. Those who enter into a group with the
idea that they can change the character of the group are
disillusioned. If there is change, it will be in the individual
alone.

Anyone—pastor, administrator, or staff person—considering the leadership role in an organization would be well
advised to give due consideration to the character of the
organization before entering service. An unhappy marriage will limit effectiveness and progress.

The history, benchmarks, and character of an organization will enable one to perceive the trends.

TRENDS

Certainly there are trends in the life and work of every
organization, and we must determine not only what the
trends are but what they mean. Where do they go? What
do they tell of the future? What do the trends mean for the
leaders? For the constituents? For the community? For the
total program for which the organization is structured?

Benchmarks, we have stated, should be steps on a staircase of progress leading to higher plateaus of service. We
all know, of course, that staircases are for ascending and
descending, to and between planes. Obviously, at times,
trends will be downward. There will be trends in both
directions, but hopefully the predominant direction will be
upward.

Administrators and administration need to discern these

trends, and they must discover how well they can relate to them personally. Some persons can adjust to downward trends without feeling a sense of personal defeat. For others, downward trends lead to personal failure.

When organizational trends are downward, those leaders who tend to be overpowered by them should avoid them. And when trends are downward, those who have the capability of accepting and adjusting to them, and sustaining courage and hope should be a part of the organization's life and work during those periods.

This is important. I cannot overemphasize this fact. Spiritual and psychological health of persons in leadership roles and proper positioning in organizational structures are imperative to organizational and individual well-being.

Trends provide keys to leadership needs and the criteria for the selection of leadership, to participants and the recruiting of members, to economy and the opportunities for expansion, and to social influence and the likelihood for service.

A survey of the trends prevailing in the organization's history will provide a picture of the cyclical aspects, and one may well determine where the organization is in the present cycle. While the major and long-term trend of an organization may be improved, it will become evident that there is a series of cyclical experiences containing both highs and lows, and it is important to know when the downward trend in a cycle is not a downward trend in the general health, strength, or projected history of a particular organization.

We have suggested that consideration be given to the history, benchmarks, character, and trends in an organization in the leadership-selection process.

LEADERSHIP

Some denominations are assisting local parishes in self-evaluation processes as one pastor leaves a parish and a nominating committee is preparing for the process of selecting another.

Occasionally churches and organizations engage in self-evaluation processes. My criticism of the process is that a group is not usually capable of objectively evaluating itself. The process requires outside, objective expertise.

Evaluation processes or organizational self-analysis ought not to be limited to those times when leadership changes. Such processes should take place periodically in an organization's life and work. The findings should be compiled, organized in interpretive form, and used in administration and programming by staff, leaders, and members.

The past is prologue to the future. Indices from the past assist leadership in the future—obviously and unavoidably. The past reveals potential for the future and guidelines for administration and leadership. One simply cannot disregard it.

14

Three Choices
Governing Administration
in the Future

In June 1978, Frank Sinatra scheduled a concert in Huntington, West Virginia. I was consulting with the Presbytery of Greenbrier of the Presbyterian Church in the United States at the time, and the concert received more than normal attention because the popular singer was detained in New York the first night the concert was scheduled and 8000 people were locked out of the city auditorium. Refunds were made to those requesting them. The following evening the concert artist appeared, and a full house gathered to hear him sing at the delayed performance.

A leader in the city of Huntington shared experiences in arrangements for the performer leading to the concert. The arrangements were detailed, complicated, and expensive.

Two bulletproof limousines were required for the artist and members in his party.

A number of police officers were to serve as bodyguards in the course of his stay.

Special carpet was installed in the dressing room, even though it was to be used for only the one evening.

The dressing room and bathroom were redecorated to

the artist's specifications. Special towels and soap were required.

Toilet paper with the performer's monogram was manufactured for the one-night stand.

Call it exaggerated public relations, if you wish, but do not overlook one very important point: Frank Sinatra was coming to town and everybody knew it!

Actually, the making of such arrangements is an important aspect of life. We know the precautions, care, and concern that accompany the visits of kings, presidents, and public leaders. Occasionally we learn of the arrangements made for ordinary people. We all know the arrangements as friends and guests enter our homes. There have always been special preparations and some initiatives that simply would not have occurred had it not been for an expected visitor.

In Asia there are things that people tend to do for their parents. In the Western world there are things that we tend to do for children and young people.

We set standards for political leaders and celebrities.

We set standards for guests, visitors, and friends.

We set standards for parents and for children.

What about God?

As we are involved in the church and its related organizations, we are about the King's business.

As persons responsible for the King's business, we should be doing a good job. After all, there is something special about God.

Nothing should be too good for Him!

Standards that the church and church-related agencies should establish for the quality and tone of the nonprofit experience revolve around three basic choices.

AUSTERITY OR AFFLUENCE

The die was cast for the Judeo-Christian experience in the Old Testament, and sustained through the primitive

Christian Era, for sacrificial offerings in an agricultural economy. Mandates required the firstling of the flock and the firstfruits of the soil. Injured or sickly animals and spotted or spoiled fruit would have been more convenient and certainly more economical for the primitive society, but neither of these was good enough.

Surely for most there were more convenient times and less costly products to share with the Deity, and certainly there were times when many contested the validity of placing God first. But this was the discipline for the Patriarchs and a practice of Jews and Christians alike for thousands of years.

It may seem unfair as we consider the various circumstances.

A young couple, early in their married life, come to spring, and the first lamb born in their limited flock is removed from their asset ledger to become a charitable contribution.

A couple with limited means come to harvest. The wait has been long, the work hard, and the environment less friendly than it might have been. The crop is not good. Grains and vegetables are not fully ripe. Damaged fruit would seem the most practical gift. But it is the firstfruits of the harvest that become the spiritual offering.

Or we consider a herdsman or farmer in the advanced years of life. The daily task has become more painful with the years, and there are fewer animals, smaller fields, and limited strength. Here, too, it is the firstling of the flock and the firstfruits of the harvest that become the oblation.

In the age of jet travel, computer technology, and condominium living, this price seems too high. The course of the religious organization is one of frugality, and annual budget appeals state or imply that support is required only for an austerity budget.

I have sat in on many meetings in literally dozens of denominational settings dealing with budgets. Frequently questions are raised as to what further reductions might be made. Seldom have persons raised the questions as to what the budget should be in terms of dollars and cents to advance ministry and mission.

Austerity in the church and church-related agencies is as much the order of the day as affluence is in the home and in the marketplace.

Every year thousands of people present their dreams to the Small Business Administration, seeking funding for new opportunities in new business ventures that will give them the privilege of sharing in the free-enterprise system. Fewer than one in twenty-five will be given the chance to carry out that dream even in initial stages. More than two thirds of them will be turned down by the administration because their budget projections are inadequate to produce the product, support the process, and bring the project to a successful conclusion.

Through the years we have seen hundreds of churches finance capital expenditures for buildings, but seldom for equipment and hardly ever for program. In fact, I cannot cite a single incident of a church financing a program without funds committed to see that program through at least what the congregation assumed was a full period of operation. Had the church been as willing to finance programs as buildings, the substance of the religious organization would be much stronger in America today.

The counsel of business is simply this: Don't go into the business unless you are willing to take the risk and expend that which will be adequate to make a proper project and effort.

There may be times for austerity budgets. However, the place of austerity budgets is not at the beginning of the budget-making process, but only at that point after which every door has been knocked on, every bell rung, and every person challenged to share generously. Only when there is no alternative.

Why are austerity budgets the order of the day for our churches and church-related agencies? Is it because people say No? Is it because people simply will not give? Is it because all folk are doing as well as they possibly can? Of course not!

The basic reason lies in the fact that a few are saying No for the many. Leaders generally are of the impression either that people will not give or that they are giving all that they can.

Each person needs to come to a personal encounter with spiritual demand. Each must decide whether he or she will give the equivalent of the firstling of the flock and the firstfruits of the land to the mission of Christ and his church. Most have never been challenged. Some never have the opportunity. Leadership's mind-set of austerity shortchanges spiritual experiences and casts doubt on expectation for mission. The leadership is saying No for others, and seldom, if ever, testing the validity of the thesis.

Individuals in an affluent society will not be content, or impressed, with the significance of the church's life and work, or its organizational function, if it is structured on austerity budgets.

Austerity or affluence? There is no choice. Standards must be consistent with daily experience and life-style.

ECONOMY OR EFFICIENCY

Economy implies a compromised efficiency. Certainly there are economic measures that are efficient, and in most cases, when the efficiency factor is determined, the economic consideration falls into a proper perspective. But most economy in the church and church-related agencies is false economy. It is not economy as a result of efficiency but economy at the expense of efficiency.

Price is the primary consideration in most eleemosynary organizations. When requisitioning supplies and services, the criterion is usually price. The most for the dollar is the basic policy.

Time also is not the important factor. The criterion is

not what will be the cheapest over a period of time, but rather what is the cheapest now. Quality is not a basic ingredient of the ecclesiological framework. The ecclesiastical environment smacks of cheapness in a society efficient in the marketplace and in the educational arena.

Economy versus efficiency is in leadership itself. In parishes where the congregants select leaders, the selection process is governed by "what we can afford" and not by "what we need." In the episcopal type of church, the criterion is "what they can afford" first and "what they need" next. In fact, what they think they can afford takes precedence over what they need in practically every situation.

This may appear to be an attack on leadership. It is not. It is an attack on the system that places skills, attributes, and needs as second best. In few places are leaders permitted to exercise their greatest skills in areas where their excellence is compatible with the situations they are required to serve.

Constantly leaders seek to adapt their skills and attributes to the situations that they are called to serve, and the challenge is to adjust to the limitations and factors of impossibility rather than capabilities and need. Leaders are selected on the basis of "what we can afford now." And the leadership is that which is acceptable for the present.

We do not need to confine these criteria to the selection processes for clergy. We discern them in every area of personnel and service in the church and church-related agencies. From the officers to the custodial services. From the organ chamber to the choir loft. From the finance office to the playground. Where there is excellence, it is the result of commitment. Economy is the hallmark of much that we do as Christians.

In the world of business, the first consideration centers on the right person for the job. Having discovered the person, his or her education, experience, and capability, a second question is, What will it cost to secure his or her services? In a few cases a job is never undertaken because resources are not projected to be available for proper staffing. The luxury of inadequate staffing to do a job is too great a luxury for the marketplace and should be considered too great a luxury in the field of religion as well.

EXPEDIENCE OR EXCELLENCE

Austerity and economy walk hand in hand with expedience. It is expedient that we have an austerity budget. It is expedient that we exercise economy in all that we do. Excellence is at home in almost every area except that of the church.

Consider excellence and organized religion. The standards for excellence in organized religion stand separate from those of the world. In fact, a standard for excellence in the church is a standard of excellence in and of itself. For the excellence in the church cannot be compared with the excellence in the secular world. As we have seen, it is generally most inadequate.

Place the criterion before any vocation, commodity, or service. When we enter the compound of mission, it simply cannot stand the test of a proper comparison to government, industry, education, or commerce.

In looking back over the history of organized religion in the United States, I believe that the mimeograph has done more to harm the church's image and degrade standards for operation throughout the entire religious enterprise than any other one thing. Innocently the church was anxious to spread the word. Mass production of printed information was simply and economically produced but with a reproduction process that was generally poor—poor in design, in typing, and in reproduction. But it was convenient. It was cheap. For the vast majority it was rated good enough.

I am personally convinced that if the Multilith had taken the place of the mimeograph, the entire image of the church as we near the end of the twentieth century would be different. More costly? Certainly. More effective? Without a doubt. The standard for religion would have changed and would be on a level of acceptance and design competitive with the marketplace.

I write this to the church's shame!

It is true that we sometimes bring affluence, efficiency, and excellence into ecclesia, not as standards of affluence, efficiency, and excellence all their own but as affluence, efficiency, and excellence contingent to commitment.

This does not mean that we degrade commitment. Certainly not. But let commitment complement the church's mission, affluence, efficiency, and excellence rather than the religious society's commitment to austerity, economy, and expedience.

Let the church's standards become the model. Let remuneration, policies, and practices for personnel provide examples to commerce and industry. Let the litany and music set the standard for the theater and the other arts. Let the instruction and education provide models for disciplines of the human mind.

"Now when Jesus was born in Bethlehem of Judea" we are told that the Holy Mother "wrapped him in swaddling clothes." It was a practice of the nobility. And out of those who would cradle a child came the very best of manhood.

Nothing should be considered too good for the King of Heaven. The church, the Bride of Christ, must become par excellence. Anything less is a mockery of the faith that we profess as Christians, for through Christ's Holy Church and its related agencies we are engaged in the King's business!

Index

DATE DUE

MAR 2 '89			